THE
AUTHENTIC
BISTROS OF PARIS

THE AUTHENTIC
BISTROS of PARIS

By François Thomazeau

Photographs by Sylvain Ageorges

Translated by Anna Moschovakis

THE LITTLE BOOKROOM
NEW YORK

Originally published as *Au Vrai Zinc Parisien*

© Editions Parigramme, Paris, France, 2004

© 2005 François Thomazeau

photos © 2005 Sylvain Ageorges

Book design: Louise Fili Ltd

Printed in China

Library of Congress Cataloging-in-Publication Data

Thomazeau, François.
The Authentic Bistros of Paris / by François Thomazeau ;
photographs by Sylvain Ageorges ; translated by Anna Moschovakis.
p. cm.
ISBN–10 1-892145-34-0   ISBN–13 978-1-892145-34-5
1. Restaurants — France — Paris — Guidebooks. I. Title.
TX907.5.F72P3776 2005
647.95443'61 — dc22   2005010359

Published by The Little Bookroom
1755 Broadway, Fifth floor, New York, NY 10019
(212) 293-1643 Fax (212) 333-5374
www.littlebookroom.com

Distributed in the UK by Macmillan Distribution Ltd.

To Catherine B., André G., Alphonse A.
and to Georges, the king of the authentic bistros of Marseilles.

F.T.

To Véronique

S.A.

On a run-down old square
In a poor part of Paris
Some angel took this dive
And made it
A palace.

GEORGES BRASSENS,
Le Bistrot

Contents

Introduction

EVERY COUNTRY HAS ITS WATERING-HOLES, EVERY CITY DRINKS IN ITS OWN WAY. IN THE SOUTH OF FRANCE, IT'S the open-air culture of the *terrasse,* and the lazy but lascivious bar scene. In the North, drinking is an indoor sport perfected at the pub. But make no mistake: the English pub is not the same as the Scottish pub, or the Irish. Each is its own type; each has its own soul.

The soul of Paris eats, drinks, and is revived in the bistros. The most brilliant chroniclers of bohemian Paris — Francis Carco, Pierre Mac Orlan, Alphonse Allais, Léo Malet, Antoine Blondin, Michel Audiard, Alphonse Boudard, Albert Simonin, Robert Giraud — all nourished their inspiration, honed their characters, and sharpened the lurid details of their plots on the fortifying meals and hard-drinking clientele that together define the spirit of the bistro.

In recent years the word "bistro," like so many others, has been diluted to death; it's now used to describe restaurants that look like bars, with distressed wood paneling, "old" countertops with fake patinas, vintage appliances dug up at flea markets, and "neo-rustic" dishes of meat and cheese. Rural charm meets urban sophistication. A cup of nostalgia in the flavor of the day.

Those aren't real bistros. The dictionary is clear enough: in French, a bistro is a bar, plain and simple. And, with a few borderline exceptions, all the establishments described here (with unabashed subjectivity) are just that: bars. But in France, a bar is more than just a bar. It's a place where the pulse of daily life keeps time to a neighborhood's rhythms, from 6 AM coffee and a glance at the morning tabloid (folded behind the counter, near the phone that still accepts coins), to the first glass of dry white wine once the *boeuf bourguignon* or *blanquette* of veal starts simmering in the kitchen. Then a parade of aperitifs; the workers' lunch at noon; the *plat du jour;* the *digestif* at 3:00; the four-o'clock lull. Afternoon coffees, hot chocolates when school lets out for the day. And the long, fluid expanse of "evening" prolonged eternally by those who, out of loneliness or preference, put off going home as long as they possibly can.

That's what a bistro is. The essence of a neighborhood's soul.

It's a far cry from a *cantine,* a *réfectoire,* or a *buvette.* Entering a bistro is like entering someone's home. And you are expected to behave like a guest; you have rights, but also responsibilities. Many a tourist to Paris has misunderstood this contract: the customer may be king, but in a real bistro there *are* no customers, only guests who are just as responsible for the ultimate success of a place as the owners and the servers are. A bistro is a relationship of equals, with the customer contributing as much as the staff. That's why you shouldn't expect a bistro owner always to be friendly. He's at home. He has a right to his moods.

Of course, the food and the drink count for something, too, but at a bistro, it's more about the men and women who spend time there, and whose souls, after they're gone, will still haunt the back rooms, the booths, and dark corners. It's about bits of conversation ricocheting off the tobacco-stained walls, little bursts of laughter, tears shared at the bar.

Most of the owners of the bistros in these pages have a single word on their lips: *soul.* They feel as if everything they've created is hanging by a thread, built on a fragile foundation of ghosts and time. Many of them told us they were afraid to expand, to repaint, to resurface mirrors that have become clouded with age, to change their tablecloths, their hours of operation, their brand of coffee. It isn't nostalgia. They're afraid they might break the spell. Afraid they might chase away the guardian angels who bring them business.

There are others, of course, who have taken the risk. Intrepid owners who have gone ahead and updated the venerable look immortalized by Robert Desnos and Willy Ronis. After all, they're in the business of serving drinks, first and foremost. And a fresh coat of paint is sometimes necessary, if only to appease the health inspectors. Some, like the new owner of La Tartine — known as the most photographed bar in Paris — have tempted fate with a complete facelift, risking the scorn of many loyalists. But we should remember that these dim, gray bars were once bright and shiny as a copper penny — just as the chiaroscuro of the old masters sometimes owes more to grime than to the talent of the artist. To those who have risked offending the purists we say *bon courage.* Time will tell.

Because bistros need time, languor, and memories. The employees don't want to have their names pinned to their blouses. To know the waitress's nickname — or the boss's — is a privilege that must be earned. It takes time. Like a patina. Sometimes a café becomes so imbued with the personality of its proprietor, people stop calling it "Le Chiquito" and it becomes, simply, Chez Roger. Sometimes, it doesn't work out that way. There are bars where you feel unwelcome, for no particular reason — and others where you feel at home, also without any reason.

Maybe it's because when you enter a bar, you become a part of it, you see it in your own image. It's not for nothing that the French term for "barfly" is "pillar", as in *pillar of the establishment.* These most loyal of loyalists may as well be attached to the counter, fastened to the booths, to the café's very structure. If they die, or stop coming around, what will be left?

Surprisingly, in the beginning, bistro meant "quick." That's what a bistro was, a sort of fast-food joint in the era when Cossacks stationed in Paris became fixtures in the city's nightlife. Others claim that the word (which comes from the Russian) gained its present meaning from the famous *"tournée des grands ducs,"* at the turn of the last century, when the Russian czar and his entourage, hosted by then-French president Sadi Carnot, indulged in an extended night of debauchery that from then on would be associated with a kind of Russo-French pub crawl, from counter to counter, stool to stool, bar to bar.

Who knows? So many legends are born in cafés, so many rumors are spread in them. So many hoaxes. So many expressions. Come to think of it, do you know what a "bar" is?

For starters, it's that long metal bar that runs the length of the counter, near the ground, which allows you to rest your feet for as long as you can prop yourself up on your elbows and give your docile attention to the regular night owls.

And a "cabaret"?

The ornate copper tray on which coffee and tea were served in Middle Eastern restaurants.

And the origin of the word *guéridon*, the round white marble table on the terrace on which you rest your elbows, car keys and a strong coffee in hand?

From one of Louis XIV's African slaves, who used to carry his master's candlesticks before setting them down on the type of table that now bears his name.

Have you heard of Mylord l'Arsouille?

In the middle of the 20th century, he was more famous than an astronaut. The illegitimate son of a minor nobleman from Brittany, he squandered his paternal fortune in just ten years of concerted drinking in Belleville's bars before going on to preside over the annual "Descente de la Courtine," the equivalent, in 1950, of a giant street rave, which attracted more than 250,000 revelers to Paris each summer.

Yes, bistros teem with legends, with loudmouths and ghosts. When absinthe was still on the menu, they could become raucous dives. But each winter, pastis brought the flavor of sunshine and summer vacation to Parisian lips.

Literary talent flourished; so did the back rooms where customers discussed and debated; so did jukeboxes and foosball. They'd sing *L'Internationale* or *Nini Peau de Chien* and play another game.

Bistro was supposed to mean "fast," and yet now these cafés serve as nonchalant soldiers in the fight to save Paris from becoming just another fast-moving, stressed-out, poorly fed capital city. How times have changed!

Suddenly, the spirit of the bistro is perpetuated by the desires of the stomach. In these pages, you'll find some bistros that aren't really bars at all, where people go to eat more than to drink. But, just as the

English have their pub food — familiar meals you swallow whole between beers — and the Spanish their *tapas,* Paris has its *bouffe de bistro,* the kind of food grandmothers prepare, slowly but not painstakingly, neither fast nor fancy. Casseroles, *blanquettes* and *bourguignons,* "house wine" (*vin de propriétaire,* as the signs often announce); some of these, like Mélac, Gouin, and Chanrion, have for decades worked to champion the taste of good country wine in the face of shifting fads and trends. And today, a growing "slow-food" movement seeks to reclaim the same magic formula — simplicity, conviviality, authenticity — that bistros have employed since the beginning.

Nostalgia aside, the fact is that the authentic Parisian bistro is a species facing extinction, like the true London pub, the Italian *trattoria,* wood-oven pizza, and the old-style *bodega.* To fill the pages that follow, it proved not to be so easy to find fifty true bistros that passed the test. Plenty of places came close: like the remarkable Le Petit Bar on rue Richard-Lenoir, with its octogenarian bar-matron barely managing to keep up the "*exotique*" decor; the cages that once housed parrots and monkeys now keep only memories behind their bars. When old women give up, a whole world dissolves.

One of the criteria we settled on was to test the ham sandwiches (*jambon-beurres*). It was an arbitrary decision, but it turned out to be revelatory. Good bars make a good *jambon-beurre.* That's just the way it is. And their beers are the right temperature. And the espresso is neither too hot nor too cold, no matter what time you order it. And the house red is never harsh.

And will we ever be able to repay the people from provincial Auvergne, who settled in Paris at the end of the 19th century and the beginning of the 20th? It may be coincidence, but a large number of the establishments we covered are or were owned by natives of that region.

The *café-charbons* have almost disappeared, as have the oil-pails and seltzer bottles, but the spirit of an unofficial pharmacy — where people once warmed their bellies with wine and their hands with coal — is still an essential ingredient of the bistro. As are the *aligot*, the *Salers* and Saint-Pourçain. The Auvergnats brought a lot to the capital. Above all, they transformed the architecture, the way of life. And they continue to do so. Far from resting on their laurels, the Auvergnats and Cantalous are helping the bistro evolve into something new. Le Costes, run by a third-generation Auvergnat, is a perfect example of this modern evolution — although you won't find it in these pages, any more than you'll find l'Ambassade d'Auvergne or La Galoche d'Aurillac, both monuments to the culture of Auvergne but more restaurants than bistros.

Recently, the flame has been passed, and many bistros of the new generation are owned by Algerians from the mountains of North Africa. Berbers, really.

The profession remains the same: a stable compound of back-breaking labor and passion. That's another reason for the progressive disappearance of the hard-core bistros. To stay open from 6 AM until 1 AM, to satisfy hunger, quench thirst, and absolve sins — it isn't a career, it's a calling. So instead we have specialization: wine bars, oyster bars, late-night bars…never mind the theme bars that usually don't last a day longer than the trend that inspired them.

But what does it matter, as long as we can continue to respect the traditions that make life a bit more worth living. The little rituals. Ice cubes that crackle in anisette; sugar lumps plucked out of small metal bowls and plunked into the bottom of an espresso cup; teeth sunk valiantly into a *jambon-beurre-cornichon* at the counter; the salt shaker emptied over a decapitated hard-boiled egg, washed down with a beer. The absence of ashtrays on the bar. And all those aperitifs with names that evoke an era and the atmosphere of an old pub. Like Proust's madeleines. The lost look of a girl sitting alone in the corner of the room. A few words from the waitress or bartender, utterly routine but somehow comforting when it's time to face going home.

As long as the dusty glow of a bistro's neon sign lights up the street at night; as long as an exhausted waiter wrapped in a black apron stacks chairs on tables of wood, marble, or formica at closing time; as long as the soul of the bistro lives on, Paris will still be Paris.

> *Every attempt has been made to insure the accuracy of the information contained in this book. However, hours and days of operation may vary from a bistro's posted hours; the reader is strongly advised to call ahead to make sure the establishment is open.*

Le Béarn

2, PLACE SAINTE-OPPORTUNE · 8, RUE DES HALLES, 1ST ARR.

☎ 01 42 36 93 35 🚇 CHÂTELET

OPEN DAILY EXCEPT SUNDAY

THIS SMALL AND UNPRETENTIOUS CAFÉ IS A RESTFUL DESTINATION AMIDST THE HUSTLE AND BUSTLE OF LES Halles. Nestled on the corner of the place Sainte-Opportune, next to the most spectacular rat exterminator's shop in Paris and not far from the beautiful Guimard entrance to the Métro, it is the perfect place to stop for a quiet drink or to eat your lunch in peace.

The former butcher's shop, which was converted to a café just after World War II, is the picture of good taste. The tiles in the entryway and behind the bar are attractive imitation art-nouveau (if you want to see the real thing, head across the Forum des Halles to Le Cochon à l'Oreille, see page 27, or to the friendly, Por-

tuguese-run Le Royal on the rue Saint-Denis).

At Le Béarn, even the faces in the photographs that surround the mirror in the back have the welcoming look of old friends. For less than ten euros you'll be served a flawless *plat du jour (pot-au-feu, escalope normande)*. The wine list

is limited but well-chosen, including Saint-Pourçain and Petit Cairanne.

Behind the bar and on the floor, the owner's daughter and a young waiter add a refreshing energy to the place. Stop in the Béarn for a shot of espresso, a quick *digestif,* or an afternoon coffee — or to set down your shopping bags for a moment before heading back out into the melee. This is a bistro to relax in.

Bistrot Victoires

THIS USED TO BE A BAR-TABAC, LE PIED DE BICHE, AND AN OLD BLACK SIGN WITH WORN METALLIC LETTERING testifies to its long-lived devotion to tobacco. After that, an ex-rugby player converted it to a gourmet Basque restaurant called the Cave du Souletin, whose reputation is still upheld by the inventive and delectable menu of the Bistrot Victoires, founded in 2003. This low-key bistro offers a savvy combination of the best elements of the past — traditional café decor, lovingly prepared country-style food (succulent ribs with toasted thyme), a discreet smoking room — and the present.

In the restaurant world, location is everything, and the Bistrot Victoires takes its identity from its topography. Hidden behind the imposing wall of the Banque de France, protected by the corner of the rue Catinat from the discriminating gazes of the fashionable Place des Victoires, it belongs to all of its adjacent neighborhoods — Palais-Royal, Les Halles, Sentier — without belonging to any of them.

Businessmen in suits and ties, clerks in training with the *conseil d'État*, tellers from the Banque de France, and lovers of good food rub shoulders with a trendy gay crowd that has recently adopted this eclectic venue. A café at a crossroads seems to have finally found its way.

Le Rubis

10, RUE DU MARCHÉ-SAINT-HONORÉ, 1ST ARR.

☎ 01 42 61 03 34 🚇 PYRAMIDES, TUILERIES

OPEN DAILY EXCEPT SATURDAY NIGHT AND SUNDAY

THE MARCHÉ-SAINT-HONORÉ HAS SEEN IT ALL. ORIGINALLY THE SITE OF AN ENORMOUS CONVENT, IT WAS TRANSformed first into a bustling covered market, then a garage for fire trucks and paddy wagons. Today, it serves as ambassador of *le bon goût français,* showcasing French luxury goods for well-heeled tourists who've come slumming from the Tuileries. In this atmosphere, it's difficult for a café to maintain its authenticity — which is what makes Le Rubis the jewel of the neighborhood. The older regulars remember drinking here in 1934, when it had a different name. At that time the market, which was built in 1810, spanned an area as big as the Forum des Halles. In 1948, Gouin opened Le Rubis, a small café dedicated to that most indispensable luxury, wine. Since then its curvy pewter bar, its single row of tables strewn with plates of ham, and its curtains (which provide a bit of privacy from the circus outside) have held their own against the winds of fashion — and the floods of *bobos* (bourgeois bohemians).

Albert Prat, who has been proprietor for some twenty years, is responsible for turning Le Rubis into a temple to Beaujolais Nouveau. On the cusp of winter, without fail, fans of the young wine form a mob scene around the barrels and wine presses set up near the door, eager to perform their annual ritual. But the boss is no fool: new is good, but old is better. Try tasting his impeccable Côtes-de-Brouilly, his irreproachable Fleurie, his gem of a Juliénas. And Le Rubis is not provincial. Just try to find another bar in Paris that serves a Rosé from Cairo.

The highlight of the menu, for sentimental reasons, has to be the *rillettes de Joëlle*, infused with its namesake's native Sarthe. And it's impossible to miss the flag from the Stadoceste Tarbais which hangs next to the door, a gift from French soccer greats Philippe Dintrans and Jean-Michel Garuet, pillars of a different community from the one that dominates the crowded bar. You may prefer to eat *à l'étage*, next to the open kitchen—an inviting sight for curious eyes.

Le Cochon à l'Oreille

15, RUE MONTMARTRE, 2ND ARR.

☎ 01 42 36 07 56   🚇 ÉTIENNE-MARCEL, LES HALLES

OPEN DAILY EXCEPT SUNDAY AND MONDAY

THE COCHON À L'OREILLE IS A DREAM OF A BISTRO, A LITTLE TREASURE IN CERAMIC, GLASS, AND WOOD. IT'S like a dollhouse, but with a bar. The Sarregueminian faience walls, which depict scenes of life at the turn of the 20th century, are officially protected national treasures. But the real scene is the room itself, and every aspect of

it deserves mention. The bar, bearing the patina of countless fingers, elbows, and coasters. And leaning up against it, a man with a scraggly beard, expressive hands, a voice thick with drink and experience. The boss, Jean-Marie, is behind the bar, with a rebellious moustache and a sparkle in his eye. And if a tourist couple, dressed to the nines, orders a Coke to go with their duck *confit*? The answer's no. Here, it's water or wine, end of story. Even though there is always a stash of Coke in the fridge: it's reserved for hangovers.

The wines are classics, too, and dependable. A deliciously fruity Chinon; a robust Vacqueyras. And the food? The menu reads like a history of local bistro fare: *Os à moelle*, pork and cabbage, thick-cut steaks fairly bleeding their juices, hot and cold sausages, cabbage. It's like a museum of the neighborhood's culinary heritage, a monument to good taste.

As wine flows from the bottles, so do the stories among the regulars, about the provinces they left to become Parisians. Real Parisians. Then it's time for a final coffee — and, all right, one more *digestif* for the road. At the Cochon à l'Oreille, the wooden chairs are unupholstered for a reason: if they were more comfortable, nobody would ever leave.

Le Croissant

IN ANY GIVEN BISTRO DURING THE LUNCH RUSH, YOU'LL HEAR A HARRIED BUSINESSMAN SHOUTING "WHERE ARE YOU?" into his cell phone, trying to locate his wife among the crowd. Everyone within earshot turns and smiles. At Le Croissant you're likely to hear a slightly different question: "Where is it?" And the response is not the usual "I'm downstairs." Not at Le Croissant. "Where is it?" ask the bankers, the journalists, and, lately, even the young hipsters. The waiter sets down his *plat du jour* to point out the table where it happened. And the window where the killer stood. "This is the table, but it was over there."

Is this a good thing or a bad thing? To have a drink or eat lunch in a historic site, frequented by former President of the European Commission Jacques Delors? Yes, Le Croissant is the bar in which Jean Jaurès was assassinated on July 30, 1914. Strange that such a place would be so popular. But it has recently been taken over by the young managers of the *café-philo* les Phares, in the Bastille, who are trying to revive its period feel.

The bar used to be called La Chope du Croissant, and in the eponymous street, which was full of printing-houses and newspaper offices, the air was filled with the specialized slang of the typesetters. The addresses alternated: a bar, a printer. Zinc counter, lead type. A glass, a page. The repetitive movements of presses and of drunks.

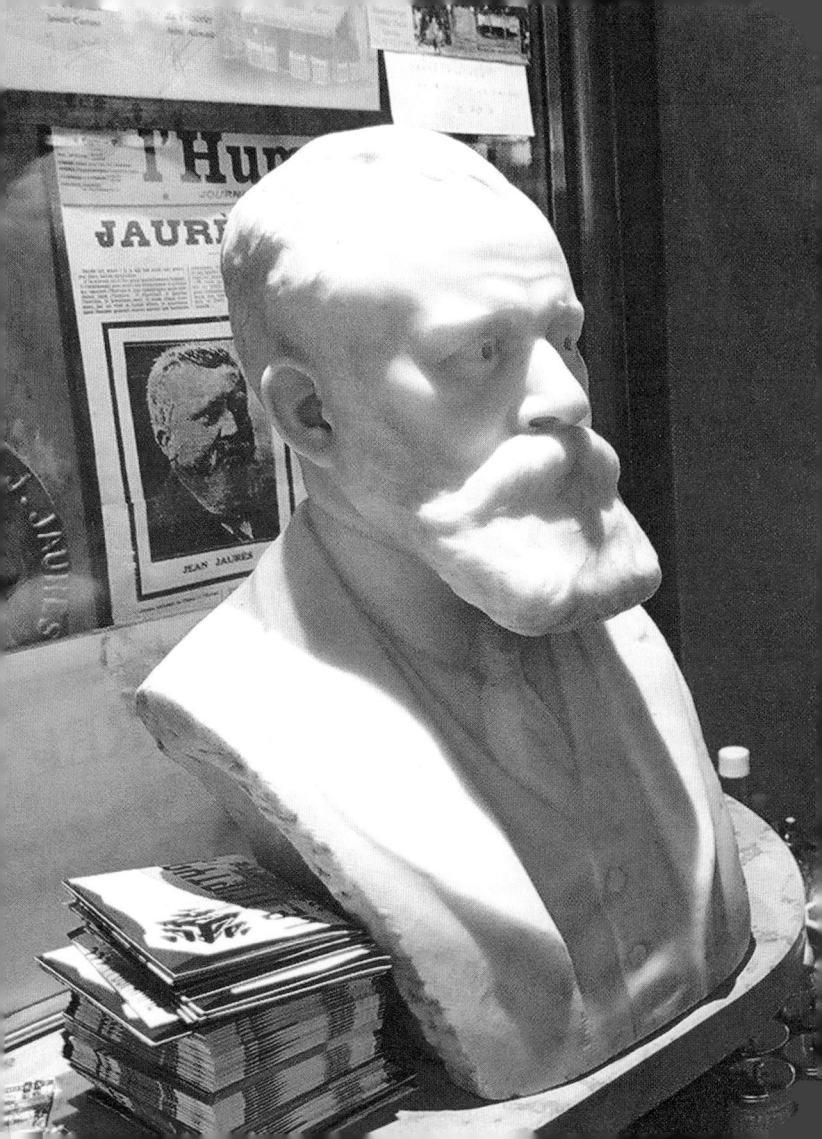

Now only Le Croissant remains, along with the remarkable Le Port d'Amsterdam, a Dutch dive barely surviving on the corner. Jaurès's wood table is still around, too, and each day it plays its part in the service of Le Croissant's delicious meals. A bust of the legendary Socialist long presided over the room, but recently it's been removed. Sign of the times: down the block, an old café has been converted into a police station.

La Grappe d'Orgueil

5, RUE DES PETITS-CARREAUX, 2ND ARR.

☎ 01 40 13 00 17   🚇 SENTIER

OPEN DAILY EXCEPT SUNDAY AFTERNOON AND MONDAY

BISTROS ABOUND IN THE QUARTIER MONTORGUEIL, BUT LA GRAPPE D'ORGUEIL STANDS OUT FROM THE REST. ITS charm goes beyond its perfect embodiment of a classic Parisian café; you'll find it working in small ways, a special touch here and there. A gentle seduction. At midday, a friendly throng arrives for lunch. In the evening, the hour of the aperitif, you have to elbow your way to the bar,

and the few tables in alcoves are coveted. But you have to sit quietly, observe, and study the clues if you want to understand what's special about the atmosphere at La Grappe.

First of all, there is very little noise (except in the evenings when the bar plays host to *raï soirées*) — no boisterous groups, no shrieking coffee machines, no headache-inducing Top-40 radio. Perhaps a discreet Chopin, perfectly suited to the wine. It should come as no surprise, in a building that once belonged to the singer Georges Moustaki. Here, people seem to have time to spare — like the passersby, who drift in as naturally as if they are a part of the atmosphere.

You learn a little more by studying the graying photos on the walls, showing La Grappe as it was two centuries ago, and the yellowed ones of handsomely coiffed gentlemen with luxurious scarves, their elbows leaning on tables bearing ornate copper platters. The grandfathers of Debia, the proprietor? Perhaps.... And suddenly, as your eye falls on the center of the bar, you understand. It's the roses! That's what makes the difference.

In a vase at the end of the bar, next to the telephone, a collar of red roses encircles a single white bloom. It's superb — and it was a gift from a regular. There are roses at the entrance, others on the partitions that separate the main dining room from the booths. Flowers are at the heart of the place. Because La Grappe d'Orgueil is a café run by a woman, and women are, without a doubt, the future of this business.

Le Petit Vendôme

8, RUE DES CAPUCINES, 2ND ARR.

☎ 01 42 61 05 88   🚇 MADELEINE, OPÉRA

OPEN DAILY EXCEPT SATURDAY AND SUNDAY

WHAT HAPPENS WHEN A BUTCHER FROM BURGUNDY MEETS A HAIRDRESSER FROM PARIS AND THEY BUY A BAKERY together? They turn it into a bistro featuring the food and wines of the Auvergne, of course! And why not? That's exactly what Christian and Patricia did, fifteen years ago, near the Place Vendôme. And even if the storefront and menu are as explicit as can be ("Auvergnat Spoken Here"), even if the Saint-Pourçain flows like water, Christian — with his strong jaw, his well-kept mustache, and his easy manner — has retained a slight accent from his native Midi. Nothing in the world of bistros is accidental. Christian was once saved by a miracle; when he was a child he almost drowned in the Fréjus dam. After swallowing all that water, it's only natural that he would devote his life to wine…Along with the Saint-Pourçain, he favors Côtes du Rhône and Beaujolais, like the rest

of the bars in the neighborhood. Yes, the casks in the window and the hams suspended above the bar are a little kitschy, but a bar's authenticity comes from its people. And at lunchtime you'll find dozens around the bar, patiently waiting their turn to savor the choice meats served up by the boss, who hasn't lost his butcher's discernment.

You do sometimes have to fight for your turn at the Petit Vendôme, but it's worth it. If it's really too full, though, you might want to try the *plat du jour* at the Royal Vendôme, just a couple of doors away. There the salads are Pantagruelian, the Brivadois proprietors are amenable, the waiters efficient and the rough-housing infamous — not to mention the wine. An old garage converted into a friendly canteen does wonders to fill the void.

Le Tambour

SOME BARS SHOULD BE ENTERED WITH AN OPEN MIND AND A JOKE AT THE READY. LE TAMBOUR IS ONE OF THOSE bars. Be forewarned: if you can't read the tone of the local repartee, the shady character behind the bar — sailor's cap, moustache — will put you instantly in your place. If he doesn't, then André Camboulas, in his woolen sweater, sideburns, and moustache (but of course), will take care of you. In some bars, the staff takes an interest in the customers. Le Tambour is one of those bars.

There are some bars where it is impolite not to speak to your neighbors, where it is perfectly acceptable to peer into the plate of the person at the next table, so you can order the same thing. It's like that at Le Tambour. At lunchtime, it was always packed as tight as the skin on a drum — until André decided he would only open in the evenings.

Before a row of dioramas constructed in old wooden wine crates, bits of homespun philosophy are doled out daily. In the back is a photograph of Neil Armstrong walking on the moon. All under the watchful gaze of Socrates. Because there are some bars in which, without any real philosophical pretensions, there's preference for the Greeks over the more commonly found busts of Maure Casanis.

In an homage to Plato's cave, no doubt, there's even a diorama of a miniature Tambour, complete with a cast of characters — so you can watch a pint-size likeness of yourself downing a pint of beer.

"Let him who would serve the world first serve himself," an old regular might declare, making a bad Socratic pun. But you can be sure that André, seizing upon the offering, will return the favor in kind.

nôtre ici-ailleurs d'urbain bucolique rêve / pensée / acte du 21 juillet 1969

Le Petit Fer à Cheval

30, RUE VIEILLE-DU-TEMPLE, 4TH ARR.

☎ 01 42 72 47 47   🚇 SAINT-PAUL

OPEN DAILY

THEY SAY GOOD THINGS COME IN THREES. THAT IS CERTAINLY THE CASE FOR XAVIER DENAMUR. IN JUST A FEW short years, he has taken over the section of the Marais around 30, rue Vieille-du-Temple, well away from the old Jewish ghetto. He owns three restaurants here: the literary café La Belle Hortense, the serious restaurant Les Philosophes — and Le Petit Fer à Cheval, a quintessential bistro. The latter, of course, is the one that touched our souls. The proprietor had the good sense not to change a thing, although the place did undergo a recent facelift. Funnily enough, the original sign still hangs over the door, proudly welcoming people to the Café du Bresil. And yet, there's not a single *caipirinha* in the house. Instead, you'll find exquisitely selected wines from small vineyards — 22 of them, to be exact. As for the décor, it's white tiles, recycled Métro benches, mirrors discreetly painted with jazz instruments, the metal wall clock — all an homage to the good old days. Hungry souls are made to feel right at home in the small dining room, which is open until evening.

And then, of course, there is the horseshoe-shaped bar that gives the bistro its name. There are very few bars like this one. Perhaps the indispensable little café on the rue du Sentier that's run by a boxer and by Marie-Jo, the queen of Silicon Sentier. Still the Petit Fer à Cheval is ideal, for its spaciousness, its layout, and its conviviality. It's the kind of bar where nobody ever turns his back on his neighbor. Even the grouchy, sleep-deprived student who's been drinking coffee in the corner will find himself drifting toward the bar, attracted as if by a beloved.

It's as if the very shape of the bar is responsible for its magnetism, and the crowds approach it at all hours of the day: at lunchtime for a helping of the delicious, neo-traditional cuisine, and in the evening for a bit of conversation. And even if you pass by La Belle Hortense across the street, and Les Philosophes next door, you'll want to stop into Le Petit Fer à Cheval. The chance to touch this lucky horseshoe shouldn't be passed up.

La Tartine

24, RUE DE RIVOLI, 4TH ARR.

☎ 01 42 72 76 85   🚇 SAINT-PAUL

OPEN DAILY

IT WAS THE MOST-PHOTOGRAPHED BAR IN PARIS. ALSO, THE MOST-VISITED BY TOURISTS—JAPANESE, ENGLISH, AMERICAN—determined to track down the bohemian Paris of their fantasies. It was also outdated, uncomfortable, and a little bit disgusting. It felt like a museum, an anachronism, frozen circa 1926 and preserved by the former owner, who finally threw in the towel in 2002 (he was in his 90s). La Tartine's charm was dependent on its nostalgia value: the idea that "Paris will always be Paris." And many wished for the legendary café to remain always the same, eternally stained by the smoke of millions of cigarettes and cigars.

The debate raged among bistro devotees. Should it be touched? Bernard Séguis, owner also of the Chai de l'Abbaye near Saint-Germain, dared to say it should. He restored the place to its original luster, gutting the insides and opening up a new entrance on the rue du Roi-de-Sicile. He kept the bar itself, unearthing some enamel flowers that had long been covered in soot. He also kept *tartines* on the menu, without which the cachet of the place would be lost, and the hanging menu boards from the 1960s, with sliding panels advertising the day's offerings.

He added a kitchen, and gave all the walls a fresh coat of paint—yellow, to approximate the original hue. From his native Aveyron, Séguis

added *aligot* and other provincial recipes to the menu.

Was he right or wrong? Will the tourists still come in droves to La Tartine now that it no longer bears the distinction that cynics called its crowning glory: "the dirtiest restrooms in all of France"? At least La Tartine is still a bar, and hasn't morphed into a boutique or a *boulangerie*, like so many of the places in this neighborhood. And that's already something.

TARTINES

JAMBON CRU

SAUCISSE SÉCHÉ

SAUCISSON D'AUVERGNE

ANDOUILLE FERMIÈRE

PATÉ - RILLETTES

BEAUFORT . ROQUEFORT

CABÉCOU - CANTAL

SAUMON FUMÉ

ASSIETTE CHARCUTIÈRE

ASSIETTE DE FROMAGES

St NECTAIRE

CROTTIN PAIN POIL. BEUR

TARTINE PAIN POILANE

Le Temps des Cerises

31, RUE DE LA CERISAIE, 4TH ARR.

☎ 01 42 72 08 63   🚇 BASTILLE, SULLY-MORLAND

OPEN DAILY EXCEPT SATURDAY AND SUNDAY

IT ALL BEGAN WITH AN ATTACK OF THE BLUES. YVES AND MICHÈLE HAD HAD ENOUGH. MICHÈLE WAS A DESIGNER WHO made accessories out of photographic negatives, and then one day — Enough! Cut! The couple had a talent and an affinity for playing host, so they thought: why not make a career of it? So they sought. And they found.

What a stroke of luck that this annex to an old Celestine monastery was available. Firmly planted on the corner of a street just a few steps

away from the Bastille, its exterior walls covered with tiny ochre ceramic tiles, Le Cantalou was just what they were looking for. It was love at first sight. A broker helped them seal the deal, and one blazing summer day in July 2003, they stepped behind the bar and began serving drinks. The takeover was so far from hostile that the former owner's daughter still works here, fighting her way through the throngs that form during the lunchtime rush (which the French call the *coup de feu*).

Yves and Michèle haven't made a lot of changes. They've just injected some youthfulness into the place, enhancing the decor with kitschy flea-market treasures. The regulars come around for a glass of red (a very good *petit Bordeaux*) or a glass of white.

The floor, covered in regulation tiles, makes you suspect a cellar below. Legend has it that this is the room where the monks would have their meals, and that when a certain sign was given, a trap door would open and a sumptuously set table would rise from the basement.

Now, the food is prepared by Victor, who dropped in one day for a drink on his way to an interview at another restaurant. Yves and Michèle were on the lookout for a chef—another stroke of luck. Sometimes, in the evening, musicians will drop by and play a few tunes. Looks like jazz has defeated the blues.

Les Pipos

2, RUE DE L'ÉCOLE-POLYTECHNIQUE, 5TH ARR.

☎ 01 43 54 11 40 Ⓜ CARDINAL-LEMOINE, MAUBERT-MUTUALITÉ

OPEN DAILY EXCEPT SUNDAYS

THE NAME MIGHT SOUND PRETENTIOUS, BUT LES PIPOS IS ANYTHING BUT. THE FAÇADE IS A REGISTERED MONUment, and, really, the whole place is a monument. Just ask the generations of students who, by the hundreds, have frayed their pants legs on these wooden stools. *Pipos* is the nickname for upperclassmen at the nearby École Polytechnique, the prestigious school that has long held a mythical place in the French imagination. And the bar has long stood here, on the corner, to provide a meeting place for the nation's elite. This spot is so entwined with the legend of the Polytechnique that some claim the *Pipos* used to climb up the small wooden spiral staircase behind the bar, strip off their plumed uniforms, and descend as civilians so they could really let loose. The party continues, though times have changed. Not Les Pipos. The legacy of an early Breton proprietor lives on in the large wood-framed mirror behind the bar and the *lit breton* in the back room which opens to reveal a rustic mural of the port de Concarneau. We're far from the sea, and from the mountains, too, despite the claims of Saint-Geneviève. But not in spirit. The Métro is far away, down in the valley; the bus doesn't climb this hill. And along with its twin across the street, the Bar de l'X, Les Pipos remains protected from fashion — and the onslaught of pedestrians. The walls tell the whole story: a portrait

of French tightrope walker and acrobat Blondin, another of cult musician Serge Gainsbourg, a poster singing the praises of Corsican wines.

On the checkered tablecloths, you'll find Auvergnat sausage, *pavé de Charolais,* runny Saint-Marcellin. At the marble bar, their feet resting comfortably on the polished-wood base, the owners of the neighborhood's most popular bars, like Le Piano Vache, share conversation with their waiters and waitresses. The crux: at Les Pipos the owner, Christophe, is soon on a first-name basis with everyone. You don't need a degree from the Polytechnique to recognize that as a good sign.

Le Verre à Pied

118 BIS, RUE MOUFFETARD, 5TH ARR.

☎ 01 43 31 15 72 🚇 CENSIER-DAUBENTON

OPEN DAILY EXCEPT SUNDAY AFTERNOON AND MONDAY

AH, LA MOUFFE...IT MUST BE SAID UP-FRONT: THIS STREET HAS LOST THE ESPRIT BISTRO. SADLY, THE CHANGES IN the rue Mouffetard only foreshadow the future of other neighborhoods in transition, like Oberkampf—which in thirty years will look just like this, a daisy-chain of tourist traps. But at least there is the Verre à Pied, which resists the trends and calls to mind the days of Bob Giraud, when La Mouffe, this "goat trail," was like "an out-of-whack conveyor belt, where you ride out the night with only your head and your fist to guide you."

Like a narrow corridor leading straight to the soul of bistros everywhere, the Verre à Pied is a vestige of the past, a reassuring flashback—from the ancient Seita cash register to the *toilettes*. Every smoker in the vicinity winds up here, leaning up against the long miniature wood bar (barely deep enough for a *"verre à pied,"* the stemmed glass for which the restaurant is named). If only the floors could talk. It's been this way since 1870, when this formerly private *passage* opened as a *café-tabac*. Posed against the large wall mirror, which makes the tiny café seem larger, a couple of students, an aging intellectual, and two local residents returning from the market are all enjoying the *plat du jour*: a *blanquette* of veal, neither too done nor too rare.

The back walls discreetly display the work of local artists, which is not nearly as bad as at most places. The tables are closer together and the conversations are louder, too. In the back, a small door suggests the presence of a courtyard. The best table is hidden behind the refrigerator. Above it, an old painting of La Mouffe as it once was makes it possible to forget the changed face of reality outside the door. To thank the proprietors who have tried so hard to remain in contact with the ghosts of Giraud and Doisneau, go on: why not have another glass? For old times' sake.

Chez Georges

11, RUE DES CANETTES, 6TH ARR.

☎ 01 43 26 79 15   🚇 MABILLON, SAINT-GERMAIN-DES-PRÉS

OPEN DAILY EXCEPT SUNDAY AND MONDAY

TUCKED AWAY ON THE RUE DES CANETTES FOR HALF A CENTURY, CHEZ GEORGES HAS BECOME AN ARCHETYPE OF the Latin Quarter wine bar as it exists in our imagination, not in present-day Paris. Except that here, it does.

The counter for which the bar is named sits like a throne in the middle of a floor that seems made to hold cigarette butts, crushed by the

heels of generations of shamelessly perpetual students. Bright-eyed, grizzly-haired old-timers surround the wooden bar (the original zinc didn't survive the Occupation), and rehash the past under the gaze, in turn bemused or blasé, of Nicole. It's a moody world, Chez Georges, with moody inhabitants.

On the floor, sitting around an eclectic array of tables — two wooden square-tops, a round marble café table, another in formica — a

veteran of the neighborhood reads *Le Parisien*, two students intensely inhale their *blondes*, two others are engrossed in a game of chess.

Once a man named Georges reigned over this little world, before deciding in 1999 that he'd had enough. There were even two Georges, the younger one behind the bar, the older working the taps.

On some nights, a nostalgic calm pervades Chez Georges, inviting you to linger over the photos of old regulars pinned up on the wall. On others, throngs of vivacious youth invade the place, recalling the buoyant Saint-Germain of long ago, which no one under sixty remembers.

But as long as there's a barfly left to plop down at the Comptoir des Canettes for a glass — or a bottle — of red, the rebellious spirit of Saint-Germain will not evaporate completely.

La Palette

43, RUE DE SEINE, 6TH ARR.

☎ 01 43 26 68 15   🚇 MABILLON, SAINT-GERMAIN-DES-PRÉS

OPEN DAILY EXCEPT SUNDAY

THIS IS A BEAUTIFUL BAR, ACROSS FROM THE BEAUX-ARTS—SO BEAUTIFUL THAT IT HAS BEEN CLASSIFIED A monument, and so classic it can seem a bit stiff. But even the counter (of shining tin) is somewhat softened by the actual painters' palettes scattered here and there, by the efforts of minor artists hanging on the walls (said to be payment-in-kind for bar tabs), and by the stunning ceramic panels in the back room—so modern, so contemporary, that it's hard to believe they are more than seventy years old. Once attributed to Foujita, they are actually the work of the art déco illustrator Maggie Salcedo.

La Palette is so beautiful it has drawn celebrity after celebrity, sometimes in pairs. Picasso and Braque, Hemingway, Catherine Deneuve and Marcello Mastroianni, Jim Morrison—all have spent time on the terrace of this historic bistro.

Of course these days, the students of the Beaux-Arts prefer to lunch down the block at L'Assignat or to play see-and-be-seen at its partner in hipness, the neo-kitsch Bar du Marché, a little further up at No. 75.

Here at La Palette you won't find any fashionably ragged twenty-somethings trying to catch each other's eye. Just some well-behaved tourists, a little frightened by the brash humor of Françoise and Charlie, or disconcerted by the organized chaos that belies the bar's efficient service.

Stationed behind her discreet cash register, Françoise watches over her domain with a hint of mischief. She fell into the bistro business at a young age, and she knows every nook and cranny of her Palette. She loves it, without a doubt. But out of restlessness, she sometimes dreams of a change; of yellow and red formica tables, 1950s transistor radios, clean lines. Everything that La Palette isn't.

Chez Léon

5, RUE DE L'ISLY, 8TH ARR.

☎ 01 43 87 42 77   🚇 HAVRE-CAUMARTIN, SAINT-LAZARE

OPEN DAILY EXCEPT SUNDAY

IF IT WEREN'T SO HARD TO PARK A TRUCK ON THIS TINY STREET, THE 50S-ERA COUNTER AT CHEZ LÉON WOULD BE lined with weary teamsters on break between runs. Except that trucks are banned in today's Paris, making the continuing existence of the city's last remaining truck stop, in the middle of the 8th *arrondissement*, all the more strange. Chez Léon (named for a long-forgotten former owner) isn't just the only truck stop in Paris — it was the first "Routiers" in all of France, and the origin of the term. It was established in 1934, the same year that the first truckers' union was formed. An aristocrat, François de Saulieu, had the inspiration to organize the union while sitting in this room, which seems to preserve the past in its decor, with its ceramic tiles, Bulle clocks from the 1920s, and swinging doors leading to the original bathrooms.

The yellow formica of the fridge and cabinets harks back to that gentler era, and if the menu at Chez Léon is far from aristocratic, it embodies the noble virtues of consistency and value that define this kind of eatery.

The current owner took over from his parents, who had run the place since the 1960s, and he is more conscious than anyone of upholding the social function of his bistro: cheap eats near the *grands magasins*.

Back in the days when François de Saulieu was broke, the management let him run a tab. Laborers from the neighborhood were offered meal plans; you can still see the drawers where their personal napkin rings were kept.

Though you probably won't find a single trucker here these days, the café is still indispensable to the students from the nearby Lycée Condorcet. Sometimes, as adults they'll return, tears in their eyes, trying to recapture the years they spent in this room that now seems frozen in time.

Le Beaujolais Drouot

To BE CALLED "MONSIEUR" IN A BISTRO IS TO HAVE EARN-ED THE TITLE AND THE PRIVILEGES THAT GO ALONG WITH it. Here, Monsieur arrives late for lunch, heads for his usual spot and begins to hold forth, doling out the first morsel of advice as soon as he's taken his seat.

At the Beaujolais Drouot, when the bargain hunters have drained their coffees and their white wines, a different type of consumer takes their place: the buyers, sellers, and *amateurs* of fine art. And in the way that sports fans will rehash a game, they rehash a sale. Elated when they've made a mint, a bit morose when they've missed out. And where better to go for celebration or solace than to the bar?

For many years, the Beaujolais Drouot was the domain of Joëlle. She lorded over it, casually calling out "*bonjour*!" and "*au revoir*!" while attending to the slim bottles of wine from small vineyards selected by Michel. He was the boss—and onetime owner of the Chai de l'Abbaye and of Panache. A discreet "Variétés Club" banner serves as a reminder of his love for sports—soccer above all, but golf, too. His domain was the tables. He would lunch late (like Monsieur), with wine merchants, sup-pliers, or friends; often with managers from other bars. It's a good thing to have a sit-down meal after the lunchtime rush; around the time when

the waitress Nathalie, her shift over, props open the door to let in some fresh air from the rue Rossini.

Michel and Joëlle sold the bar recently, to pursue other adventures. But the new owner, Daniel, has preserved its spirit. He also sits down to eat while the art dealers hold their debriefing sessions. And as for the impeccable *plats du jour — brandade, tête de veau* — he never misses a step. That should come as no surprise: such experts as Monsieur wouldn't waste their time on a fake.

Le Général La Fayette

52, RUE LA FAYETTE, 9TH ARR.

☎ 01 47 70 59 08 🚇 CADET, LE PELETIER

OPEN DAILY

HEL-LO, LA FAYETTE! YES, YOU WILL FIND AMERICANS AT LE GÉNÉRAL LA FAYETTE—IT'S THE PRICE OF SUCCESS. Le Général La Fayette is an institution. But if the Americans disappeared, well, this bistro would remain the same: a flagship in permanent drydock (and open from 10 AM to 4 AM) at the intersection of the street that shares its name and the rue du Faubourg-Montmartre.

Le Général La Fayette has opted for the look of light wood (think varnished pine) with green accents—and this at a time when most brasseries trying to fake authenticity lean toward mahogany and vermilion.

The exquisite staff speaks English like Robert Dalban in the 1963 film *Les Tontons Flingueurs*.

This is an ideal bistro for lunching, dining, or drinking alone. Small tables, scattered throughout the room, make perfect lookout posts for spying on the neighborhood youth—and on the bronzed foreigners consulting their *Lonely Planet* guides.

The Général La Fayette is one of Paris's "convertible cafés." A ray of sun appears, and suddenly, you're on the terrace! You can recognize the real regulars of this establishment easily: they position their chairs with two legs in the room, two on the sidewalk.

This is a bar where you can eat and a restaurant where you can drink. Not one of those places where a sea of tablecloths lets you know if you're not dining you may as well go elsewhere. And not the kind of place that tells you, Sorry, the cook's gone for the day.

Opened in 1896, Le Général La Fayette was a pioneer among Parisian *bars à bières*. At least it was the first to offer Guinness on tap. Need we say more? Renovated and expanded by the newest owner, Michel Planchon, at the dawn of the millennium, it has evolved with grace.

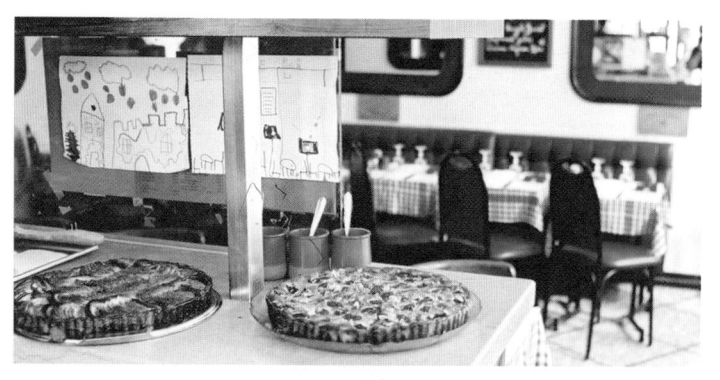

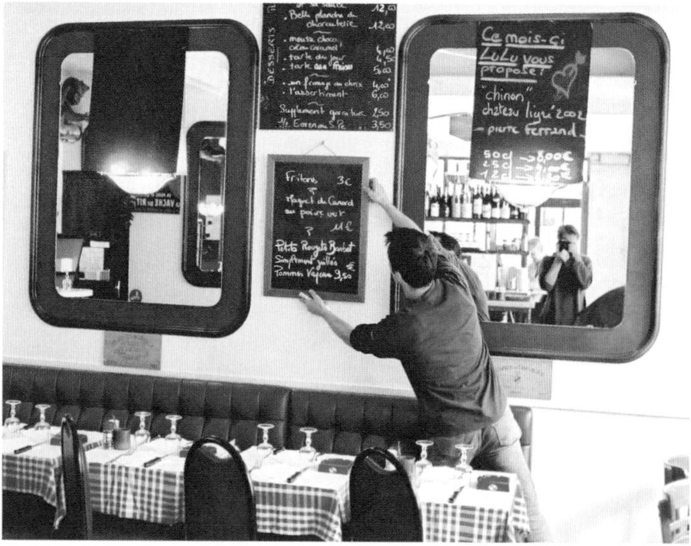
DESSERTS
Belle planche de charcuterie 12,00
mousse choco 4,00
tarte du jour 4,50
l'assortiment 6,00
Supplement garniture 2,50
3,50
Ce mois-ci
LuLu vous propose
"chinon"
pierre ferrand
50cl 8,00€
Fritons 3€
Magret de Canard au poivre vert
Petits Rougets Barbet
Simplement grillés
9,50€

Le Laffitte

IT'S A STRIKING THING: AT LE LAFFITTE, PEOPLE SMILE. OVER THEIR MORNING COFFEE. DURING THE HAPPY CHAOS OF THE lunch hour. In the evening, sipping an aperitif. It isn't that they have nowhere else to go. They are here because they like it.

"Make yourself at home!" shouts Olivier, the boss, wearing a casually hip gray T-shirt and a sparkle in his eyes. With a background working at Brasserie Bofinger, among other fine establishments, Olivier bought this old café at the end of the last century with a simple purpose: to share his love of food and drink. "Food is very intimate; what you make enters into another person's body," he says. It's true, and calls to mind an old proprietor of Le Laffitte who, motivated no doubt by hygienic concerns, would wipe the whole place down with disinfectant in preparation for Émile Zola's frequent dinnertime visits.

Le Laffitte is a hangout, a second home. You sit down and a glass awaits you — a Chinon, or a Côteaux-du-Lyonnais — with some slices of sausage, a little chorizo. It's worth coming at 12:30, during the lunch rush, to hear Olivier yell *Salut, les amies!* and continue his balancing act while his wife, Claude, tends bar: "Seat a party of four, serve a glass of wine, add up a bill, deliver a side of sausage and an espresso." Lulu, the post-punk-rock waiter, sets down copious servings of delicious food. The

meat is extraordinary. The wine is abundant. Next to the kitchen, yellowed publicity posters evoke the faded glory of a forgotten accordionist, Claude's father.

After the *plat du jour*, you won't get a selection of cheese on a plate; a platter of cheeses is set down on your table. Serve yourself... The cheeses are specially aged by Lulu, first on his balcony and then in the cellar. With care. And love.

In the evenings, it's calmer. The construction noises that have plagued the 9th *arrondissement* since the '70s take a rest. The offices close, the streets begin to breathe. You take your time deciding between the bar, the sidewalk, the small terrace. A breath, a few beers.... Curtain.

La Patache

60, RUE DE LANCRY, 10TH ARR.

☎ 01 42 08 14 35 🚇 JACQUES-BONSERGENT

OPEN DAILY FROM 6 PM, UNLESS IT'S CLOSED...

ON FIRST VISITING LA PATACHE, YOU THINK TO YOURSELF, I'VE MET FRIENDLIER PROPRIETORS THAN THE dour-looking *Père* Vito. Maybe he's having a bad day? But no, you go back a second time, and he's still scowling...That's just the way he is. It's his character, and it's part of the character of his bar. Vito has his expressions and his moods, and that's just the way it is. True, some people find it annoying that such a venerable café, with its wooden tables, its

old heating stove, its boxes filled with notes written by customers, is owned by a person with such an ungenerous character.

But that is what makes a bistro a bistro: the people who work there, and the people who eat there. And you'll have to admit that at La Patache, the stools that line the bar are damned comfortable, as are the unmatched chairs strewn about. La Patache was here long before the inevitable *bobo* invasion of the Canal St.-Martin, and finding it

required some effort in the days before the (admittedly very pleasant) Hôtel du Nord appeared out of nowhere to transform the neighborhood.

In the early days of La Patache, people would meet here for an aperitif before heading to the (now defunct) Gigot for dinner, only to return to La Patache at meal's end. Since then, of course, a lot of water has passed under the locks, and you can savor a fine bottle at Le Verre Volé, for example, or have a glass at L'Atmosphère. But La Patache is still La Patache, and Vito is as grouchy as ever.

You might be excused for thinking that it's a pose, that he's playing a role — like the famous actors who drop in now and again, spiking the night's reveries with a dose of fantasy.

La Petite Porte

HERE'S A NEW TAKE ON AN OLD TRADITION. BACK IN THE MID-NINETEENTH CENTURY, WHEN THEATERS WERE filled to capacity, they were always flanked by eateries: each theater had an adjoining tap room, canteen, or bistro where the public could have a meal or a drink before curtain time, or convene for a post-show discussion. Now, after a long intervening period of dreary decline, the area that stretches between Boulevard Montmartre and La République is seeing a burgeoning revival of such spots; they appear suddenly, like strange mushrooms sprung from the fertile streets. But instead of opening up next to thriving theaters, they now flank near-defunct porno houses and arcades. The pioneer of the trend (unless you count the eternal Gymnase) is La Petite Porte, so named for the small door, now blocked off, that used

to open up directly into the adjoining Théâtre de la Renaissance at intermission. One morning in December of 2000, the first customers pushed open the door of this little café in the shadows of the looming Porte Saint-Martin. Since then, hundreds of others have followed. It began when

three musicians, Jean-Michel, Bouli, and Thierry, were sitting around an ancient bar surrounded by fading frescoes of forgotten plays, and they decided to set aside their instruments in favor of espresso machines, beer taps, and sandwiches. With a splash of Morgon and a dash of good cheer, the special alchemy reserved for bars was achieved — like a good jam session between friends, when magic happens.

From the start, this cheerful new room, crammed up against a stage, seems as if it has been here forever, brightening up the neighborhood. On the terrace, conversations sizzle beneath the heat lamps. The owners never fail to keep their sense of humor when things get hectic, and the waitresses are as delicious as the famous *tartines*. (The secret to the latter is the bread they use, made with fresh spring water by L'Autre Boulanger.) The reason for the palpable good mood around here? All of the above.

Le Bistrot du Peintre

116, AVENUE LEDRU-ROLLIN, 11TH ARR.

☎ 01 47 00 34 39   🚇 LEDRU-ROLLIN, VOLTAIRE

OPEN DAILY

WHEN THE BASTILLE WAS STILL KNOWN AS LA BASTOCHE, THE BISTROT DU PEINTRE WAS CALLED LE SAUMUR. IT was the neighborhood bar on the corner of the rue de Charonne and avenue Ledru-Rollin that nobody much noticed anymore.

But there were painters in this building well before the massive influx of artists and galleries transformed the rue de Charonne. In fact, artists had a hand in creating this beautiful corner café — and the *Inventaire supplémentaire des monuments historiques* isn't exaggerating when it calls the façade the most beautiful example of the Moderne style in Paris.

When Hervé bought the Saumur, he and his team renovated everything, from the curvilinear framed mirrors partly hidden behind the liquor bottles to the ceramic wall pieces dedicated to two of the four seasons that flank the mirror in the back. (Before the War, there had been two others, but "Winter" and "Fall," which once held court behind the bar, fell victim to the Occupation.)

Here and there you'll still catch glimpses of the long history of the establishment: on an outdoor column, a handwritten sign puts the price of a *café* at 30 centimes, recalling a time well before prices were figured in euros.

The customers seem to have been beautified as much as the space. Young mothers lunch at round café tables next to the windows. Students loiter in couples on the terrace, and the new locals sit at the bar to indulge in the home-style meals that are the mainstay of bistros: *blanquette* of veal, washed down with a Saint-Joseph of irreproachable quality.

At night, the Bastille gets busy reinventing the world, as in 1789. But its inhabitants, no longer young, have grown as soft as the neighborhood. You almost suspect that the Seine has been diverted down to the basin of the Bastille and that you're actually on the Left Bank.

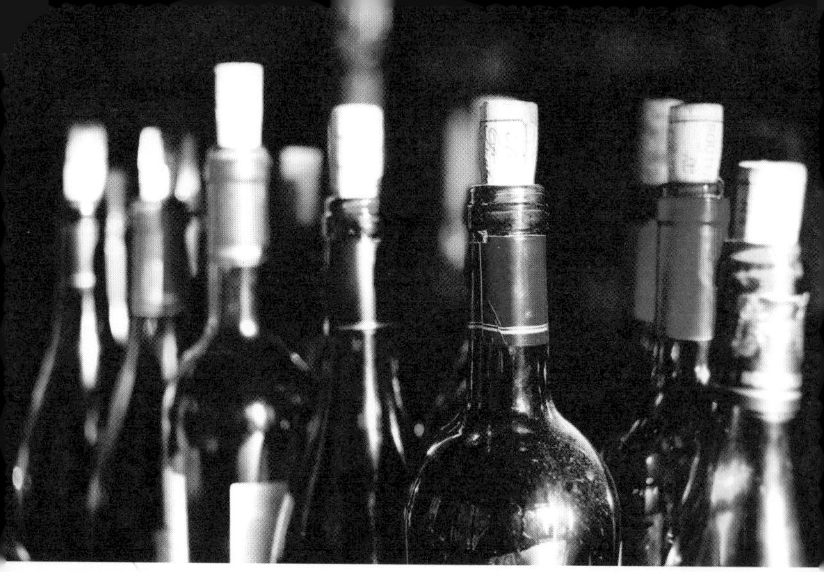

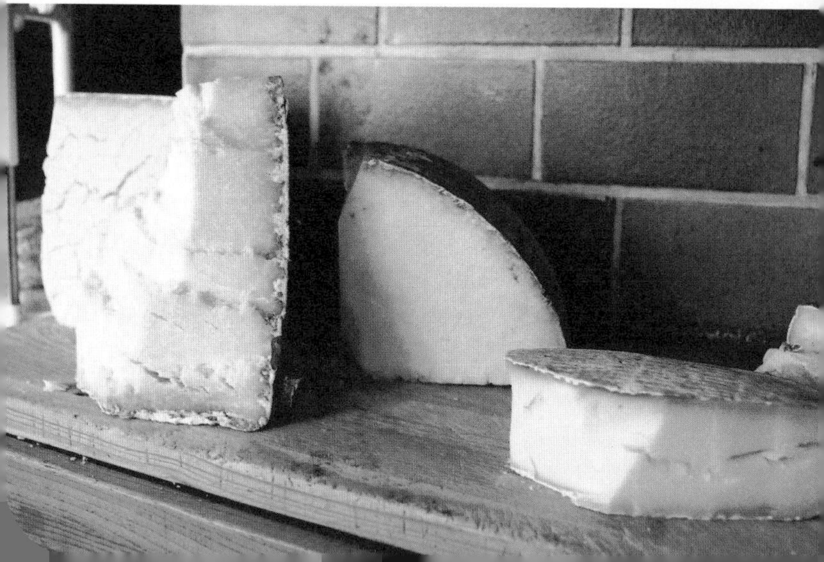

Bistrot Mélac

42, RUE LÉON-FROT, 11TH ARR.

☎ 01 43 70 59 27   🚇 CHARONNE

OPEN DAILY EXCEPT SUNDAY

IF JACQUES MÉLAC HAD APPLIED FOR A PATENT, HE WOULD BE A MILLIONAIRE BY NOW. NOT THAT HE HAS ANYTHING TO complain about; his renown has earned him mention in guidebooks from as far away as Japan. But now that wine bars — with their free-range chickens, their chalkboard menus, and their *pots lyonnais* — are almost as common as Irish bars, it's time to give Mélac his due.

For all intents and purposes, he invented the concept, along with two or three other visionaries. Since then it has been shamelessly copied, down to the mustache: since Mélac had a mustache, every self-respecting wine seller had to grow one. To say nothing of anti-globalization activist José Bové.

So, you eat organic bread? At the Bistrot Mélac, they've been serving the now-trendy *pain Moisan* for 20 years. You want local wines? The ones that put the overrated Bordeaux and pricey Burgundies to shame? Guess who rehabilitated le Cairanne, le Cotes-du-ventoux, and le Corbières?

You think two packs a day, a drunk driver, or pollution are more likely to kill you than a steak? At the Bistrot Mélac a *pavé* isn't just a thicker steak, it's a *pavé:* a hunk of bloody beef that you have to attack from all angles.

It's all about the servers here — smiles and black T-shirts with their

"Say No to Water" slogans — but it's really all about the boss. His way of moving from table to table, making each customer feel like a friend, with a special relationship to this place, a position of privilege. It's a talent that can't be taught. It's innate. And it's clear where it came from: his father, who created Le Palais du Vin in 1938, died falling down the stairs into his wine cellar, a bottle of Chablis in his hand. Passionate to the end.

Charbon Escalier

6, RUE ÉMILE-LEPEU, 11TH ARR.

☎ 01 43 71 56 18   🚇 CHARONNE

OPEN DAILY EXCEPT SUNDAY

ODETTE ESCALIER HAS SAID IT HERSELF: "THERE MUST BE OTHERS." AND YET, AS HARD AS WE LOOKED, THERE aren't. This is officially the last *café-charbon* in Paris, just steps from the Bistrot Mélac: two Auvergnat success stories in this forgotten *passage*, named for a former proprietor.

As far as Odette, who has been here since 1959, can recall, this has always been an eatery, just one of the innumerable establishments where Muscadet warmed the belly while coal warmed the building. Coal *(charbon)* was so important at the time when Odette and her husband bought the business (which must date back to the 1930s), their storeroom would fall prey to organized crime if they didn't keep their guard up.

"There's a time and a place for everything," muses Odette, well aware that a chapter has been closed. And yet she maintains that coal is better than electricity if you want to heat a space evenly. She isn't the only one. Her bistro is a meeting-place for old men from Aveyron and Cantal who play

rummy and hold forth with humor tinged by nostalgia for the way cafés used to be. The workers from the Citroën shop across the way come by, too — to throw one back between oil changes.

Because at Odette's place, the prices, too, are from another era (sixty *centimes d'euro* for a glass of Muscadet served at the counter). And she swears that as soon as her stock of coal is depleted, she'll stop. When that happens, Paris will miss her warmth.

Le Clown Bar

114, RUE AMELOT, 11TH ARR.

☎ 01 43 55 87 35 🚇 FILLES-DU-CALVAIRE

OPEN DAILY EXCEPT SUNDAY LUNCH

JOE VITTE IS A SAD CLOWN. NOT THAT BUSINESS IS BAD. NO. BUT FROM EVERY WALL OF HIS LANDMARK BISTRO, clowns look out with that exaggerated smile that always seems to hide a tinge of melancholy. Could it be their influence? Joe has designed an irreproachable menu full of delectable and imaginative dishes, of wines from small vineyards (the fruity Madiran is superb…); he seems nostalgic for an era he never quite knew. He's spent 15 years behind the bar at this annex to the Cirque d'Hiver but he's heard tell of an earlier, revered time, when the bistro was more than a place to eat and drink. It was a way of life, a meeting-place, an audition.

Le Clown Bar was for a long time the rendezvous for circus clowns from around the world. They would cross the threshold and find agents, impresarios, retired clowns looking a little worse for wear. If one of the latter failed to show up when expected, they would send out a delegation to his house to make sure he wasn't dead. Some literally made it their home: the three clowns in the black-and-white photos hanging in the front room lived upstairs.

But this is no longer the era of comedians — at least, not intentional comedians — and next door, at the Bouglione, even the artists have a tendency to eat quickly, with their fingers, while standing at the bar.

For the moment, Joe has given up on sodas, morning coffee, and afternoon aperitifs, as a way of avoiding the really depressing clowns—the locals whose red noses are the handiwork of nature, not art. But what he dreams of rediscovering is a way to recreate the spirit that once breathed through this marvelous place, noon and night. Of making the magic last.

Le Clown Bar isn't about to disappear. Joe is the fifth owner since 1902, when the establishment is first noted in the city register. But the bar, conceived by a certain Jean-Baptiste Ménéry, most likely existed before that time, perhaps even before the Cirque d'Hiver. Just imagine all the stories that have been spilled over this old bar, where clowns have been laying down their noses for a century and a half.

Le Lèche Vin

13, RUE DAVAL, 11TH ARR.

☎ 01 43 55 98 91 🚆 BASTILLE, BRÉGUET-SABIN

OPEN DAILY

THEIR PRAYERS HAVE BEEN ANSWERED. A PATRON SAINT OF BISTRO BARFLIES — SAINT ÉMILION OR SAINT LANDELIN — has heard them. An accidental turn down the rue de la Roquette or the rue de Lappe might make those nostalgic for the old days of la Bastoche turn to drink — if only to blot out the tide of renovations that has forever transformed the bars where everyone once knew their names.

The indestructible Galoche d'Aurillac is still here, and Chez Paul. But Le Zorro and Le Phiphy's are gone. La Rotonde, completely transformed. Le Bastide, abandoned. But Le Lèche Vin has not fallen to the curse of The Desertion of the Bastille. Because while other establishments opted for more dubious forms of protection, Le Lèche Vin has chosen, since it opened in 1990, the most blessed (and provocative) of protectors — religion. From the Holy Virgin who welcomes arriving revelers, to the hundreds of icons pinned up on the dimly lit walls, this is an establishment that is well watched over. The pious images

have a looming presence, and susceptible customers might experience a sudden attack of guilt as they order another round. But the young clientele persists in its heresy, and continues to worship the bottle in lieu of the cross.

It all becomes clear when you head to the *toilettes*, which have been turned into elaborate temples to the carnal pleasures. Finally, a corner carved out for Saint Amour. It's enough to give ideas to the young revelers exiting in pairs into the dark night.

Le Baron Bouge

1, RUE THÉOPHILE-ROUSSEL, 12TH ARR.

☎ 01 43 43 14 32   🚇 LEDRU-ROLLIN

OPEN DAILY EXCEPT SUNDAY AFTERNOON AND MONDAY

ONE COULD DEFENSIBLY ARGUE THAT BOURGEOIS BOHE-MIANISM WAS BORN AT THE PLACE D'ALIGRE, ABOUT 20 years ago. Which is exactly when Le Baron Bouge came along. Yes, despite the scarlet paint, it's the Baron Bouge, not Rouge. But what does it matter: everyone says "Le Baron," anyway, and the red is as much in the glasses as on the woodwork. Maybe the "*bouge*" comes from the old French adage that recommends drinking white wine before red: "*Blanc sur rouge, rien ne bouge; rouge sur blanc, tout fout le camp.*" ("White before red, happy to bed; red before white, up all night.") At Le Baron, you'll find white (Le Petit Quincy, a classic Ardoise that goes down easy) and red: Le Petit Régnié is a mainstay, because Le Baron wisely remembered the time of great Beaujolais.

Yes, the *bobo* spirit was born not far from here. One Sunday morning, in the early 1980s, they arrived, swarming around the covered market: young Parisians in knit hats and corduroy jackets, wearing their reinvented urbane authenticity on their sleeves.

Le Baron was born for them (as was Les Crocs, the nearby restaurant at 1, rue de Cotte). What's on offer? Three tables and a few chairs scattered around a bar. Charcuterie plate for less than ten euros. Some blackboards, some casks, wine served to go. And a certain attitude. Oddly, now that the *bobos* of the neighborhood are more bourgeois than bohemian, their presence is less felt in the local establishments. Le Baron has managed to forge its own identity, in the margins of the neighborhood, yet very much at its heart. It's got a bit of an attitude, come to think of it. Just like the aviator who shares its name.

Le Bihan Café

4, RUE DE BERCY, 12TH ARR.

☎ 01 40 19 09 95 🚇 COUR-SAINT-ÉMILION

OPEN DAILY EXCEPT SATURDAY LUNCH AND MONDAY AFTERNOON

IN 1913, MARIUS SOLIGNAC OPENED A CAFÉ AT 4, RUE DE BERCY. IN 2003, BIHAN GUILLAUME CELEBRATED ITS 90TH birthday. He served seas of wine, miles of Auvergnat sausage. And so what if Bihan is from Brittany and not Auvergne? By taking over this rudderless ship at the turn of the millennium, he came to the rescue of a neighborhood on the verge of shipwreck.

But the revival of Bercy began calmly, without undue nostalgia. For decades, the nearby square had served as a paradise of cheap wine, a meeting-place open 24 hours a day, 7 seven days a week, for the consumption of industrial reds made weak and cheap to satisfy the needs of the French working class.

At the Bihan, you'll find good table wine — today's popular small vintages, made with passion, with love. That love is reciprocated by diners and drinkers who know what they want. So the menu at Le Bihan is both resolutely traditional and decidedly modern. Cured meats, *tête de veau*, and tripe, accompanied by a Cairanne, a Faugères, a Syrah.

In 1910, during the Paris flood, the Seine gave this wine district a good washing. At 4, rue de Bercy, the water rose to the second floor. The whole street was resurfaced and raised, but this building stayed put, like a solitary boat stuck in the sand. The remains of the original cobblestone street were transformed into an elegant sunken terrace; in the evening, the bar takes on the feel of a wine cellar. Let the flood commence.

Le Bistrot Paul Bert

18, RUE PAUL-BERT, 12TH ARR.

☎ 01 43 72 24 01   🚇 CHARONNE, FAIDHERBE-CHALIGNY

OPEN DAILY EXCEPT SUNDAY AND MONDAY

THANKS IN PART TO THIS EPONYMOUS BISTRO, THE RUE PAUL-BERT HAS BEEN REVIVED AS AN ANTI-FAST-FOOD bastion, a little fort protecting the cult of good food. When he took over a near-defunct couscous joint in this formerly bustling restaurant district — home to the legendary Chardenoux and the venerable À Sousceyrac — Bertrand Auboyneau infused it with the bistro spirit.

Bertrand, who was the owner of Les Voyageurs, in the Bastille district, had wanted to find an old bistro. Instead he wound up here, across the street from Chardenoux, which was in need of some fresh blood. It was 1998. Other places sprang up — Le Square Trousseau, Le Vieux Chêne, L'Ami Pierre — between here and the Bastille, and before he knew it Bertrand had launched a revival of bistro food, a clear triumph over the other brand of eatery, the kind that serves small portions with a large check.

What's his passion? The best ingredients, first and foremost. A

butcher friend at the Marché Saint-Quentin; a direct line to the Breton supplier for his oyster-bar annex, Écailler. The Paul Bert has slowly replaced its early, overly ambitious menu with simple but inventive offerings that spoil your taste buds without spoiling your budget: a lunchtime prix fixe menu of 14 euros includes appetizer, main course, and dessert.

There are more than 400 wines on the list, with an emphasis on the Burgundies that tend to scare away novices. But there is also Cairanne de Richaud, the centerpiece of the Côtes-du-Rhône revival. Following his instincts, Bertrand has avoided every pitfall.

The food at Paul Bert is so good that it attracts all kinds of luminaries from the culinary world: the former owner of the Astier, the manager of the Repaire de Cartouche, even the stars of the new Slow Food movement, a socio-ecological-gastronomical phenomenon that originated in Italy. Now, it's true that the Paul Bert is the kind of bistro that's designed more for having a meal than having a drink; so after dinner, head down the street to down a last glass of Morgon at La Liberté, a tiny neo-anarchist place that serves up surprisingly good wines for very little.

Chez Gladines

FOR 15 YEARS, A PLACE CALLED THE ESPACE SUD-OUEST, IN MONTPARNASSE, HAS EARNED THE DEVOTION OF HORDES of students with empty purses and empty stomachs. But its founder, "Papa," got his start here, so it must be worth a visit. Chez Gladines (named for a former owner) is not the Rolls Royce of Basque restaurants — there are other contenders for that honor, like L'Ami Jean — but in the Butte-aux-Cailles, a neighborhood slowly being reduced to a shadow of its former self by gentrification and the *bobo* invasion, Chez Gladines remains a haven of stability.

As far back as anyone can remember, lunchtime here attracts throngs of locals, drawn by the generously portioned salads and *plats du jour*. The service is cool, quick, and efficient, and contributes to the no-nonsense appeal of the place.

When the rush is over, Chez Gladines remains a great place to observe the neighborhood, which is struggling to balance its newfound reputation with the desire of its residents for a little peace and quiet. During the afternoon lull, a drink at the bar is supremely relaxing. But in the evening, after the second seating, a young crowd still searching for its identity overruns the place, downing beer after beer before finally heading out into the night.

EUSKADI
HENDAYE
64
— PAS D'ACHAT, PAS DE BONHEUR
justice sociale?
GREVE GENERALE!
TOTAL

Au Vin des Rues

To call your establishment AU VIN DES RUES IS TO put your money where your mouth is—or where your liver is, depending on how you look at it. *Le vin des rues* was the book by Bob Giraud and Robert Doisneau (published by Denoël fifty years ago) that more or less established the canon of authentic Parisian bistros. Since that golden age, the city's true-blue bistros have been protecting their territory. But if this is war, Au Vin des Rues on rue Boulard is admirably defending its post.

Choosing such a name is a serious challenge that this place meets by offering a selection of wines from both large and small vineyards, focusing on Beaujolais and amply fulfilling Robert Doisneau's command: "Serve them truth serum, and untie their tongues." The Lyonnais-influenced menu is made to satisfy the stomach while seducing the mouth. Lyonnais sausage, *pommes à l'huile* (of course), *andouillette du Beaujolais, poulet à l'écrevisse, quenelles.* The menu, written by hand on a traditional

slate, changes so fast it can make your head spin (or perhaps that's the wine…).

On Thursday nights, they party here the way they used to in the good old days, helped along by an accordionist. The bravest diners raise their voices in song, and you begin to see the connection between the bistro tradition and the karaoke fad. So the old café (Le Petit Robinson, the decades-long enterprise of Louison and Louisette) that abdicated its walls to this pioneer of the bistro revival gets to revel again in the refrains of its era. And even the blasé hipsters who rode out the transition between the founder, Jean Chanrion, and his admirable successor, Didier Gaillard, without blinking, can't help but start humming under their breath. In early 2004 the torch was passed to the former chef Laurent, a friendly giant from Toulouse. He'll have no trouble keeping the pace.

Aux Cent Kilos

AH, THE 15TH ARRONDISSEMENT! IS IT STILL PARIS, OR IS IT AN INDEPENDENT VILLAGE, GRAFTED ONTO THE great capital? In this provincial hideout, far from the grumblings of the Métro (it's served by bus routes #89 and #95), lies an enclave within an enclave: the Parc Georges Brassens, where once upon a time, in the Vaugirard butchery, horses were regularly slaughtered.

One of their heads survived and is now perched on the frontispiece over the door that once served as the gate to a butcher's paradise. Not much remains of the old slaughterhouse, just the occasional vestige. And Cent Kilos, a café that is worth its weight in gold. There are photos of the place that date back to the beginning of the 20th century. It already bore its name, an homage to the workers at Les Halles, who would routinely carry 100 pounds of meat at a time.

A scale by the entrance offers to weigh people as soon as they turn the corner (of rue des Morillons and rue Brancion). It's like watching an old black-and-white comedy while eating your lunch. Here comes the parade: a drunkard who's dropped his bottle; an officer of the Salvation Army; a fellow gunning by in his Gordini, polluting the air and making the windows tremble; the street kids making fun of him.

The Cent Kilos is a café in transition. But rather than try to follow every trend, it's finding its own way to success. The kitchen is open from 6 AM to 2 AM; morning-coffee drinkers give way to afternoon beer drinkers, and in the evenings a young crowd appears to savor the dishes from the neo-classic menu — *pavé de l'Aubrac, blanquette de Saint-Jacques* — or bend over books of poems. When new management took over the café four years ago, they could have tried to pander to the young and hip, make a theme bar. "But it's easier to come up with a theme than to stay truc to your soul," says Cédric from behind the bar. He's not kidding.

Au Roi du Café

59, RUE LECOURBE, 15TH ARR.

☎ 01 47 34 48 50 🚇 SÈVRES-LECOURBE, VOLONTAIRES

OPEN DAILY

AU ROI DU CAFÉ SITS QUIETLY BUT REGALLY ON THE CORNER OF THE RUE LECOURBE AND THE RUE DES VOLONTAIRES. It's protected from rain, sun, and the tumult of the road by a black curtain, which also hides it from the eyes of the curious. The way things are going, its reign is far from over.

It's an unscientific poll, but one Sunday in December, at lunchtime, the door is pushed open 47 times, and more than half of those who enter are women. They grab a copy of *Le Parisien* from a stack on the counter and read their horoscopes while sipping a *café*. When they leave, the door closes softly behind them. Legend has it that this bistro served as the set for *Quatorze Juillet*, a 1933 film by René Clair. Not surprising.

The Roi du Café is almost too beautiful to be real. The look is so classic — varnished wood panels showing the patina of time, pink neon sign above the bar, original zinc counter, elegant café tables on a cozy terrace, polished wood tables in the dining room, ceramic roses on the wall, vintage posters advertising some forgotten aperitif, like Byrrh — that you

suspect it's been renovated. But no, Au Roi du Café is just showing you its real face. The staff, too: attentive waitresses in black aprons, solicitous manager behind the register, jolly barman at the beer taps and coffee machine.

Above all, the king of cafés plays the role of enlightened despot admirably, from 9 AM until 2 AM, and everyone who lives in this quiet little corner of the 15th *arrondissement*, not far from the above-ground Métro, winds up here at one point or another. For a coffee, an aperitif, a *plat du jour* as honest as it is affordable, for beer on the terrace, or just to shoot the breeze. It's a real meeting place, a place to stop by or settle in, a melting pot for a whole neighborhood of Paris. Long live the king!

Aux Sportifs Réunis

75, RUE BRANCION, 15TH ARR.

☎ 01 48 28 61 00   🚇 CONVENTION, PORTE-DE-VANVES

HOURS VARY

SPORTS CAFÉS OCCUPY A SPECIAL PLACE IN BISTRO MYTH-OLOGY. OFTEN THE ONLY ATHLETIC THING ABOUT THEM is their name. Unless lifting one's glass can be considered a sport, in which case records are being made every day. But that's about it.

And yet a few of these establishments are for real. Aux Sportifs Réunis is one of them. No other bistro could be the stage for this scene: a brisk October morning, you're knocking on the door, in vain, and next to you (knocking also) is Pierre Fulla, ex-European champion weightlifter and unlikely TV star of the Winter Olympics in Nagano. Here, it could happen. Boxing and bars have always had a lot in common. They're fascinating and intimidating: noble arts with bad reputations.

Jean (Yanek) Walczak, for one, has never let down his guard — in the ring, or behind the bar. For the initiated, 75, rue Brancion is Chez Walczak, period. The mythical proprietor is one of the symbols, along with soccer star Raymond Kopa, of the Polish immigration. Son of a miner, born in Noeux-les-Mines, Walczak became French champion in 1948 and went on to fight Cerdan and Sugar Ray Robinson before opening his bar in 1954, in what was at the time the paradise of Fort des Halles. He knew how to play host to night owls and insomniacs, and when he was ready to go to sleep he'd lie down on the bench behind the bar.

His sons, one of whom became a champion ping-pong player, have picked up where he left off, although the opening hours now vary. The dining room still serves as a temple to the glory of the noble art, strewn with photos and forgotten names from the fights of the last century. The regulars, who reserve their tables in advance, crowd into the room as if it's a championship round. And it's true that it takes muscle to pack in the plates full of meat and to send whole bottles of red wine down the hatch — like downing an opponent between the ropes.

Le Bréguet

72, RUE FALGUIÈRE, 15TH ARR.

☎ 01 42 79 97 00 🚇 PASTEUR

OPEN DAILY

THIS IS THE KIND OF BAR YOU THINK EXISTS ONLY OUT- SIDE OF PARIS. A REAL HOME-AWAY-FROM-HOME FOR THE young and lonely. But the 15th *arrondissement* has always had a provincial quality: that's part of its charm. Le Bréguet opened here, in the mid-1990s, as a stark alternative to the old Baribal, which was getting a little too bourgeois. Along with Le Cristal on avenue de Suffren (opened a bit later by the same owners), Le Bréguet shines like a beacon in the neighborhood's lackluster nightlife.

Le Bréguet is a bar without flourishes, without snobbery, without

history: on weeknights it's packed with students and young freelancers who don't have the desire or the means to go elsewhere. It's also where they go to have a drink, to plan a party, to decide what film to go see. And the best place for a nightcap on the way home.

Though it's just an ordinary bar, Le Bréguet does have a few special traits worth mentioning: on Saturday nights, it's nearly empty. The neighborhood's youth have ventured into the city — to Montparnasse or Saint-Germain. But on your average weeknight, the bar's filled to capacity — a real phenomenon.

Over ten successful years, the bar has been renovated a bit by its proprietors (four guys from the provinces, of course), and the changing exhibits keep it from getting stale. Theme nights are sometimes planned, since live music is frowned on by the quiet neighborhood's silent majority. But the essential activity at Le Bréguet is the simplest: have a cold one with friends, and let the time go by.

Le Café Antoine

HECTOR GUIMARD IS BEST KNOWN FOR THE ENTRANCES HE DESIGNED FOR THE MÉTRO. BUT THE ENTRÉES AT Café Antoine are just as admirable. Guimard designed this little bistro in a pocket of the 16th *arrondissement* that was home for him and all his curving, spiraling art-nouveau furniture.

At Café Antoine, the *pavés* and the sausages have the rebounding curves of a Guimard façade, and this napkin-sized place, which has hardly changed since it opened in 1911, is as crowded at lunch as the Métro at rush hour.

People settle in all along the tiled wall, adorned with roses and edged in a shade of green that, yes, makes one think of the colors of the Métro.

Antoine was the first owner, who ran the place until his death, when his daughter took over the reins. Since then, Angelo has officiated behind the bar and on the floor. With a smile as bright as his polished counter, he shores up the defenses of Good Taste, keeping a keen eye on everything, including the mix of sedate locals, half-lit regulars, and tourists searching for authenticity.

Angelo has altered very little, other than restoring the curved bar to its pre-war luster — the original zinc one having been stolen during the Occupation and replaced with plastic — an all-too-common occurrence.

Behind the golden coffee machine and throughout the room, old copper etchings depict sporting scenes: a racetrack, a regatta on the Marne.

In the evenings, once the silverware has been put away, some of the eminent figures of this peaceful neighborhood drop in for a drink. The old Gaston, the voices from Radio France, a TV reporter, and lots of faces that seem *so* familiar. For the moment, they are concerned with one thing only: a last drink, to prolong the sweet night.

LAITCHAUD

TELEPHONE

Le Cyrano

3, RUE BIOT, 17TH ARR.

☎ 01 45 22 53 34   🚇 PLACE DE CLICHY

OPEN DAILY EXCEPT SUNDAY

IDEALLY SITUATED BEHIND THE PLACE DE CLICHY, LE CYRANO IS PROTECTED JUST ENOUGH FROM THE STREET'S UPROAR. Take a turn at the corner brasserie, another at the reference library, and *voilà!* There it is, as obvious as a nose in the middle of a face.

It seems to have originated as an add-on to the theater next door, L'Européen. And it's still a great place to wind down before the curtain goes up, and, before you settle into your seat, to settle your stomach with the copious *tartines* served at all hours. Whether you're seated at the bar or at the red formica tables across from it, your gaze will be drawn by the golden mosaics on the walls, by the deco details that sometimes go overboard, and by the mixture of good and bad taste that gives the place its charm. Edmond Rostand created Cyrano on the boulevards, but it's here, in this little room bathed in sunlight every afternoon, that his spirit endures.

On each of the four walls of the café, naïve paintings (a bit worse for wear) illustrate the exploits of that gentleman from Bergerac. A strain of bluesy music escapes from the radio, and for a moment you believe it must be coming from the French horn suspended above the bathroom door. The rattan upright-bass case behind the bar seems to offer a response to the complete indifference of the clientele of college students, bureaucrats, and fading stars of the stage. Under the previous owner, Jackie, soccer pennants flew next to the bric-a-brac, and the Baron, an old aristocrat and ex-dancer at Michou, gladly extolled the good old days. It should come as no surprise that this conglomeration of ideas, of characters and décor would have appealed to the Surrealists: Breton, Éluard, and Soupaient all drank here.

The new boss, formerly of Le Tambour, has retired the pennants but not the eccentric signage that is the real legacy of his predecessors. Want to know the exchange rate between the euro and the old French franc? Easy. It's written on the ceiling. Just lift up your nose.

L'Alibi

L'ALIBI. AT FIRST, YOUR ATTENTION IS CAUGHT BY THE STRANGE NAME. BUT THEN IT BEGINS TO MAKE SENSE when you hear a regular at the other end of the counter having an argument on his cell phone: *"Allô, chérie?*…Yes, I'm here. We have a bad connection….I'm on my way home…" Two hours later, the poor guy orders his sixth glass of lager or amber, glances at his watch and mutters, "Oh, *zut….*"

Ah, L'Alibi! It's a funny little night spot that appeared on a quiet corner in the 18th *arrondissement* in 1992. It's run in such a casual way that it's sometimes hard to tell if it's open. It seems always to be in progress: a touchup of the green paint on the front door; another coat of cream-gray going up on the walls. So you might wonder about the origin of the faded "vieux tabac" mural which seems to suggest that they haven't changed a thing here since the days before bistros discovered renovation. Unless…the walls do seem to be even grayer than they should be, as if an inspired artist has rubbed them down with charcoal.

It's a simple place, L'Alibi: 85% of its business is beer on tap. Saint-Omer, for a provincial accent. The old Murphy pump is there strictly for looks. Most customers, male and female, favor leather jackets. Hairstyles are unisex, too: either much too long or much too short. The speakers

broadcast obscure jazz, forgotten blues: the kind of music you listen to on vinyl.

The star, as usual, is the owner-bartender. Pascal has bright eyes and messy hair, and he performs an amazing balancing act. Change the record, serve five beers, three coffees, and two glasses of red. Take a gulp of Perrier, make fresh ice cubes, wash the glasses first in cold water, then in hot.... Makes you wonder what *his* alibi is. His mother probably thinks he's on tour with the band.

Au Bon Coin

49, RUE DES CLOŸS, 18TH ARR.

☎ 01 46 06 91 36 🚇 JULES-JOFFRIN

OPEN DAILY EXCEPT WEDNESDAY EVENING, SATURDAY

LUNCH, AND SUNDAY

JEAN-LOUIS AND SYLVAIN COULDN'T DECIDE WHAT TO DO. PEOPLE HAD ADVISED THEM: "IF YOU REDECORATE, YOU'LL have a shot at the Michelin Guide." In the end, they did nothing. This couple from the Aveyron was afraid. Afraid that if they gutted the place, if they painted over the walls which had been privy to so much laughter, so much good conversation, they would "kill the spirit of the Bon Coin." So they left it the way it was.

So the bar is a little out of date: think 1950s pinks and whites. It channels the spirit of the mother, Jeanine, who renovated when she inherited the *café-charbon* from her father, Adrian, in 1954.

Just look around. It's noon and the tables are full. The people look friendly. Nobody's trying to devour a sandwich at the counter or pay for a burger with a student meal ticket. No, at the Bon Coin, the faces are round, even rosy. People who eat *bourguignon, boudin, aveyronnais* sausage. They address Maria, the inveterate waitress, with their gravelly voices and their teasing smiles.

As for the wine, it's Jean-Louis who decides, of course. Attentive and knowledgeable, he manages to accommodate your cravings within his tastes: mostly Gaillac reds from Chez Issarly, or white Saint-Servan. It's no accident that he was awarded the "Bouteille d'or" in 2000 for his selection.

What Jean-Louis has done to keep up with the changing tides is to open up not one but two specialty shops nearby. So people can take a bit of Au Bon Coin home with them.

In the morning, where the rue Montcalm meets the rue des Cloÿs, a lantern comes on to greet the new day. Moms and dads from the nearby school stop in for their morning coffees. In the distance, you can hear the voices of their children being let out for recess.

Au Rêve

89, RUE CAULAINCOURT, 18TH ARR.

☎ 01 46 06 20 87 🚇 LAMARCK-CAULAINCOURT

OPEN DAILY EXCEPT SUNDAY AND MONDAY

NOBODY KNOWS WHAT ELYETTE'S DREAM IS. THERE ARE THINGS YOU SIMPLY DON'T ASK A LADY. ELYETTE ISN'T young anymore, that's for sure, but she still wears heels — and uses them, to shut the wooden fridge doors with a swift kick. And behind the modest barrier of a pair of glasses, her eyes sparkle with the energy fueled by four decades of bartending. Those forty years began when she was very young, before she inherited the bar from her mother. A hereditary dream, you might say. Be prepared: when you enter this dream of a bistro that now belongs to her, Elyette will welcome you as if to her own kitchen, her private space. So don't expect her to run around attending to your every need. She's more likely to give you a kiss hello, if she knows you, and to ask after your health or your grandkids.

If you coax her, she'll talk to you about the writer Marcel Aymé, who made Au Rêve his second home; she'll also tell you about Jacques Brel, who once sat on the terrace gazing up at Suzanne Gabriello's window, praying silently, "*Ne me quittez pas.*"

Then, she'll head back to her cluttered kitchen to dream up a plate of meats or cheeses, garnished with dried fruits and nuts she's cracked herself.

TAXIPHONE

1 METTEZ UN JETON DANS LA FENTE CI-DESSUS

2 DÉCROCHEZ

ATTENDEZ LE

BOURDONNEMENT

COMPOSEZ LE

NUMÉRO

3 A QUAND VOUS ENTENDREZ VOTRE CORRESPONDANT ENFONCEZ LE BOUTON A

4 EN CAS DE "NON REPONSE" OU DE " PAS LIBRE" RACCROCHEZ LE RÉCEPTEUR ET VOTRE ARGENT VOUS SERA REMBOURSE.

COMPAGNIE

LE TAXIPHONE

Buvette Boivin

14, RUE GERMAIN-PILON, 18TH ARR.

☎ 01 42 64 38 69   🚇 PIGALLE

OPEN DAILY EXCEPT SUNDAY

THE CONVERSATION IS FLOWING AT THE BOIVIN, BUT HOW CAN THERE BE ANYTHING BUT PERFECT CONSENSUS around a wine called Les Collines de la Moure, which Yves Boivin recommends to you over the pricier and more prestigious brands listed on the chalkboards behind the bar.

His Buvette, an island of safety for castaways from the drunken boat that is Pigalle, doesn't affect the pretentious (and passé) airs of so many wine bars. Not a single barrel in sight. No artificial vines or ostentatious corkscrews. Just a simple diploma, at the left of the entrance, made out to a customer for "service rendered to viticulture."

"What did he do?" you might ask.

"He drank," is the response from someone in the know, who glances up to contemplate a yellowed photo of a forgotten boxer on the wall.

At the bar, a well-known singer talks with a writer of well-known slogans. Are they members of the chorus that meets here occasionally? Are they reminiscing about the old *épicerie* that used to be here, before it was a café-theater for 20 years? Who knows? Yves is a stoic bartender, who only interferes in a conversation when it's necessary, to fill in a lull or to suggest a new subject to replace an exhausted one. But if someone mentions accordions, his eyes light up, his tongue loosens, and he rummages through his cassettes. Then, over a glass of *petit vin des Cévennes*, he invites his guests to compare the merits of Jo Privat and Tony Murena. There's no doubt that *"ça groove"*…The glasses are refilled, and two hours later, when the debaters have had their fill, the conversation stops. Yves doesn't interfere this time. The old Art Deco clock whispers tick-tock. It's time to go home.

Chez Ammad

18, RUE VÉRON, 18TH ARR.

☎ 01 46 06 40 99 🚇 ABBESSES, BLANCHE

OPEN DAILY EXCEPT SUNDAY

THERE'S A TELLTALE WAY TO DISTINGUISH A BAR THAT'S FAKING IT FROM ONE THAT HAS EARNED A PERMANENT place on the block after serving thousands of glasses of pastis: it's all in the nomenclature. On the façade of 18, rue Véron hangs a sign for the "Hôtel de Clermont." It still operates as a hotel, but it's a café first and foremost. And the boss wasn't born in Clermont but in Kabylia.

He's called Ammad. And so is his café. Makes sense, right? And yet, how many bars usurp the name of an ex-proprietor, or even use a made-up one? Not Chez Ammad. Subterfuge has no place here. There are two other signs of this bar's special status as an island of salubrity in an area of the Abbesses that is descending quickly into self-mockery. One: He gives away drinks. Not at first, and not all the time. But often. He's just following a tradition of Christian charity: this building was once a sanctuary for the indigent poor, run by nuns. Outside, a plaster Virgin Mary who's lost her hands watches benevolently over the *toilettes*, tucked away from view in of one of the miniature courtyards that the neighborhood's short streets create.

PANEFIEU
ET
AUBERT

Two: Another man who would knock you out for free, Marcel Cerdan, used to stop by for a drink with Édith Piaf when they were in love. His boxing gym was at No. 18 — right next door. Their preferred room in the hotel may still be there (all the way in the back).

In the winter, the place feels like a steam room, and you have to wipe the condensation from the window to see a colorful crowd drinking several shades of beers, happy to pass up the familiar scene down the road in Pigalle, or up in Montmartre. Some painters, some soon-to-be-award-winning writers, an old hotelier, and always a lot of great faces.

Often, instead of going out to eat, they stick around. And Ammad heads over to the stove. "You could have warned me!" he cries. Then he heats up a couscous or a *bourguignon*, and gives it away.

La Chope de Château Rouge

IT ALL BEGAN WITH A SIMPLE COINCIDENCE. ONCE UPON A TIME, FOLLOWING THE KABYLE TRADITION, YAHIA WOULD offer complimentary couscous to his customers on Muslim holidays. And then one weekend in 1995, the Christian and Muslim calendars coincided, declaring holidays on the same day. Yahia concluded that it wasn't right to offer couscous for one and not the other. So since then, every Friday and Saturday the couscous is free at this ancient Montmartre café, which according to the record books has always been called La Chope.

In winter, people come to warm up in the big, gray, neon-lit dining room. In summer, with its doors opened wide onto the sidewalk, La Chope attracts starving students: more than 400 plates of couscous are served in three seatings. So the bar has become a gathering point for unwashed youth: a crossroads between the foot of Montmartre, where hip-hop reigns, and the heart of the 18th *arrondissement*, with its modest rents and pretty girls. Most of La Chope's customers don't tan in summer and don't ski in winter; they bring their own records for the stereo. When it gets too crowded, they migrate across the street to the Clair de Lune, an older, more working-class bar. For Yahia, the unprecedented success of his bar has made him consider sacrificing the five hotel rooms he keeps on the second floor. If he did, he could double his capacity at serving time.

La Divette de Montmartre

136, RUE MARCADET, 18TH ARR.

☎ 01 46 06 19 64   🚇 LAMARCK-CAULAINCOURT

OPEN DAILY EXCEPT SUNDAY

WHEN PARISIANS HEAR "BISTRO," THEY THINK OF WRITERS LIKE BLONDIN, CARCO...BUT WHAT ABOUT THE CARtoonists Renaud or Margerin? If a real bar could be hatched from *their* imagination, it would be the Divette de Montmartre. For two decades now, this bar's been sharing its special take on things.

For one thing, it's a *bar-tabac*, and by definition *bar-tabacs* are public places in the extreme, where most of the customers are just passing through. With all that coming and going, it's hard to establish an ambiance or a sense of continuity.

For another, it's a bar full of kids. At least, it used to be. Fifteen years ago, La Divette was the headquarters of alternative rock, the second home of the band Mano Negra, and of Manu Chao — when he wasn't at the Merle Moqueur, on another hill, at the other end of Paris. And if the regulars have gone a little gray since then, it's still a rock bar, one part nostalgic, one part eternally hip. It's a bar where the music is so loud it bounces off the mirror, which reflects the celebrities peering out from the picture CDs hung on the walls and ceiling. A bar where Elvis is waiting for you in the bathroom, and the silhouette of Jacques Brel can be traced in the smoky windows. To make matters worse, they show soccer on the big screen. And if *that's* not enough to kill the ambiance, conversations taking place anywhere near the entrance have to compete with the sounds of the foosball players whacking plastic balls into metal goals. And yet, all this combines to give the place its soul. The colorful bric-a-brac and kitsch decor follow a strange logic that begins to make sense once you've had a few beers.

Serge, the imposing owner, shuttles back and forth from one end of the bar to the other. Thanks to him La Divette has remained what it is, when so many other legendary rock bars — Le Zorro, Le Baragouin — have long since taken their last drag.

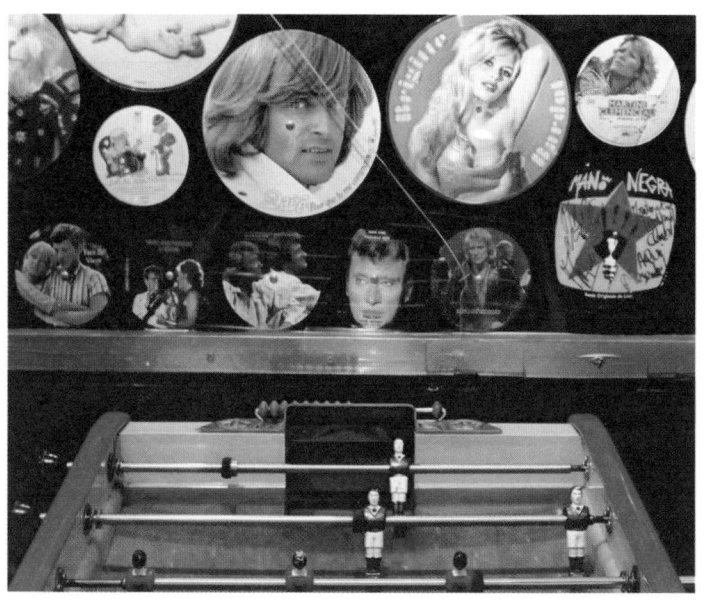

La Pomponnette

42, RUE LEPIC, 18TH ARR.

☎ 01 46 06 08 36   🚇 ABBESSES, BLANCHE

OPEN DAILY EXCEPT SUNDAY AND MONDAY LUNCH

IT WAS A STORMY SPRING EVENING AT LA POMPONNETTE. A TERRIBLE THUNDERSTORM, A HAMMERING OF HAIL. THE microclimate of Montmartre. The residents of the neighborhood arrived looking like ghosts; they bellied up to the bar, clutched onto familiar wood, plopped down on benches, and sat down at tables — vague silhouettes of artists lacking funds and sleep, casting a grim eye at the swollen sky.

That night La Pomponnette became a refuge again, as it had been in the 1920s when the illustrator Francisque Poulbot used the building to shelter runaways and abandoned kids from the neighborhood. The benevolent artist even set up a medical clinic in the courtyard. Nobody knows what happened to the *"poulbots."* Maybe they ran into each other years later having a beer at La Pomponnette…If they did, they would have struck up the bar's legendary drinking song which, loosely translated, goes: "Better drunk and hung over than boring and sober." But rest assured, it's unlikely you'll get bored (or sick) in this lofty establishment in the Republic of Montmartre.

Pass through the bar, and the place opens up into a fashionable restaurant with humorous sketches on the wall. The menu is nothing to laugh at, though. It's filled with classic offerings that sacrifice nothing to fashion. The service is assiduous, with enough ad-libbing to rouse even a

tired working stiff. But that's not why they come here, where the check is still totaled up on a little desk in the center of the room. Handwritten, just like the prescriptions at Poulbot's clinic.

La Renaissance

112, RUE CHAMPIONNET, 18TH ARR.

☎ 01 46 06 01 76   🚇 JULES-JOFFRIN

OPEN DAILY EXCEPT SATURDAY EVENING AND SUNDAY

IT MIGHT AS WELL BE THE CORNER IMMORTALIZED IN CHARLES TRÉNET'S CLASSIC SONG OF NOSTALGIA, "COIN DE rue." With a terrace on one side and a picket fence on the other, it opens up onto the rue du Poteau, a perfect slice of Paris *bobo* leading directly to the center of the 18th, by way of the marketplace. Along the terrace, the rue Championnet descends toward Barbès on the left and climbs toward Montmartre on the right. The bar occupies the crossroads, and so does its clientele. Young inhabitants of the old brick houses of Clignancourt share tables with freelancers taking a break between films. The neighborhood workforce also includes aging hipsters, more or less artistic, who are becoming the dominant population of a neighborhood in transition. They eat simple, Pantagruelian salads.

But inside, it's a whole different story: perhaps the most beautiful barroom in all of Paris. A model of the genre, with Art Deco stained glass, beautifully aged walls, pristine vinyl upholstery, dark-wood tables, a working soda-pump, and sunlight so intense it makes the dust particles dance and your eyes blink.

It's as if nothing has really changed since the turn of the last century, when Henriette took over the bar, married the waiter, and installed herself behind the marble counter, where she stayed until 1974.

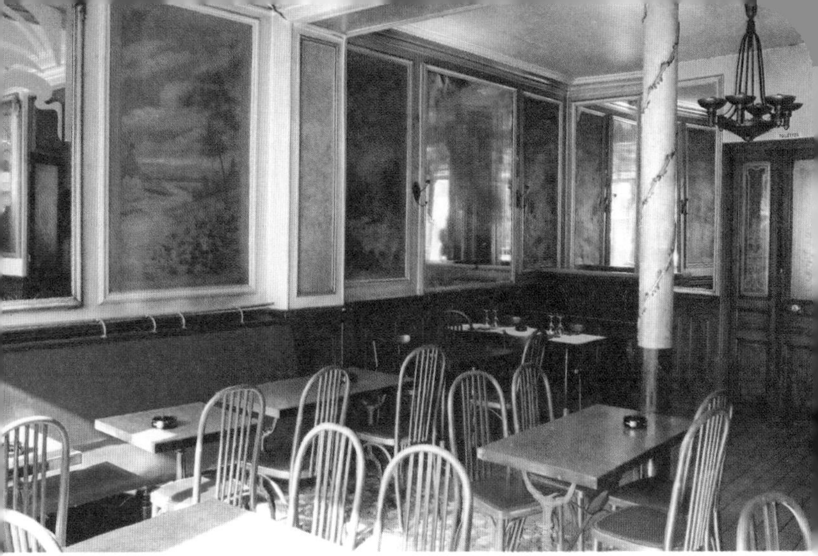

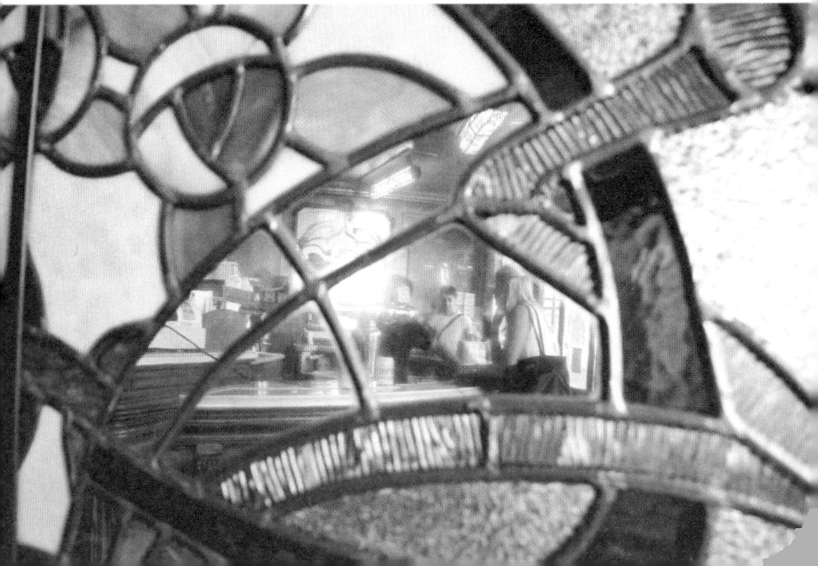

At that time it was a quiet little bistro, out of the way, ideally situated between the pimps' Montmartre and the showmen's Saint-Ouen. Discreet men, Corsicans, and gypsies with no acknowledged profession, would meet here to chew the fat — and to enjoy the single *plat du jour* on offer.

The next owner changed the name. He was a cardsharp who was much more interested in his next set of wheels than in redecorating his recent acquisition, so nothing much changed. The current owner notes that if this bar were in the Latin Quarter, it would have made the Historic Register long ago.

But who needs registers? It's the movies that make history. With this decor, in this location, it's no wonder the cameras began to show up. The comedy *Le Ripoux* immortalized La Renaissance in the 1980s, but other films have followed suit at regular intervals. On the façade, gold letters announce that you're at "Chez Jean." They look real as real can be. But they're only the handiwork of the set painter on a movie that was just filmed here.

Bar Fleuri

1, RUE DU PLATEAU, 19TH ARR.

☎ 01 42 08 13 38 🚇 BUTTES-CHAUMONT

OPEN DAILY EXCEPT SUNDAY

MADAME HUGUETTE HAD A HEN. A PET HEN, NOT YOUR GENERIC BIRD. BUT NOT A FANCY BIRD EITHER, JUST A good hen, the kind that doesn't demand very much. In the yard of the Bar Fleuri, Huguette's hen spent many a happy day. She would welcome customers with a friendly cackle, like her boss, and she was utterly oblivious of the ceramic roses for which the bar was named.

The idyll ended on September 11, like collateral damage of the tragedy that played out thousands of miles from this little bistro stuck in the 19th *arrondissement* and the 19th century. While the planes flew into those far-away towers, the customers of the Bar Fleuri, mostly journalists, got on the phone. Or listened to the radio. Or fixed their eyes on the TV. One of them forgot to keep an eye on his dog. And that was the end of Huguette's hen.

That moment unleashed a chain of events. Huguette, who had kept bar here for so long, who'd seen Alain Resnais shoot "*On connait la chanson*" ("Same Old Song") here, hung up her apron. But she still comes by for her afternoon coffee — and to retell the story of her hen.

The fable has a happy ending. One day, a pretty young woman from fancier parts wandered into the Bar Fleuri. She fell under the charm of the place, of Huguette, of the hen, of the old-fashioned flowered tiles, the decades of *plats du jour* eaten and the gallons of wine consumed. When Huguette retired, the pretty woman dropped everything so she could follow her heart. Because there are still beautiful princesses in the Kingdom of Bistros. With her brother Mathias at the bar and the stove, and the romantic landscape of the Buttes-Chaumont just a few steps away, she's living the real-life fairy tale of the hen who laid a golden egg.

- Oeuf dur mayonnaise t
- Rilletes de la Sarthe
- Paté Breton
- Saucisson sec
- Jambon de pays
- Salade mixte (sala

- Bavette à l'échalote
- Entrecôte poëlée

Le Café Parisien

2, PLACE RHIN-ET-DANUBE, 19TH ARR.

☎ 01 42 06 02 75 🚇 DANUBE

OPEN DAILY EXCEPT SUNDAY

BEFORE MICHEL TOOK OVER THIS LITTLE SPOT THAT ONCE BORDERED A HORSE MARKET, THEN A HOSPITAL, LE CAFÉ Parisien didn't have a name. The locals always called it by the owner's first name. Then Michel came along in 1989 and added "*parisien*" above the sliding glass doors. Because even if this neighborhood is sometimes known as "l'Amérique" (thanks to the flourishing of certain businesses that supposedly export all their profit overseas), even if you can take a short walk to Mouzaïa and think you've stumbled on a forgotten battleground in Algeria, it would be hard to be more Parisian than this café.

The terrace that opens onto the square: Parisian. The walls, which Michel has tiled in the classic style of Métro stations: Parisian. And the regular customers from all over the world who arrive at all hours and belly up to their favorite spot at the bar, leaving the mark of repeated contact on its surface: Parisian.

The neighborhood (a part of the 19th from which you can't really see the huge gray buildings that appeared out of nowhere in the 1980s), the area known as Mouzaïa, with its cobblestoned alleys and postcard-perfect streetlamps: Parisian.

And above all Michel, who directs the activity of his little world from behind the bar: Parisian. Strong-armed and good-humored, Michel

goes with the vintage Hollywood décor like pastis goes with water. The movies wouldn't miss it for the world. It's so Parisian, this bar, that Delon filmed here — and so have some of the season's television hits. And the guidebooks have taken notice, recommending this timeless spot to their readers. Michel couldn't care less: the only things you'll find on his window are an old faded sticker and a crack where a ball lost its way.

He takes pride in the fact that one of the most typical bistro drinks, le Picon, comes from his native Algeria — from Oran, to be precise, where Gaëton Picon invented African bitters. You can learn that every night, chez Michel.

Lou Pascalou & La Boulangerie

14, RUE DES PANOYAUX, 20TH ARR.

☎ 01 46 36 78 10   🚇 MÉNILMONTANT

OPEN DAILY

ONCE UPON A TIME, JUST OFF THE RUE DES PANOYAUX, AT THE BOTTOM OF MÉNILMUCHE, THERE WAS A LITTLE street so out of the way that you expected to see Mme Piaf the elder hanging her laundry. A cobblestoned street, with lampposts, a dry goods store, a bakery. A timeless apparition amid the towering affordable housing units with their high-security gates.

The little street has its bistro, too, of course — an ancient former post office that survived by the grace of God. You almost expect someone to start unloading a stage-coach. In the evening the lights are on full strength; it feels a little like a toy store. When Momo's father arrived from Kabylia, he swore that one day he'd buy this bar. The son has kept the father's word.

Momo, the owner of Lou Pascalou, transformed the municipal architecture with a cinema-ready décor including walls the color of cardboard. Whether on the terrace, or in the spacious seating area that hums with conversation, you're encouraged to warm up before settling down to eat. Or after…

After a few beers, if you listen closely you'll hear the sound of a flute. Follow it. Where could it lead but to a bakery? And it does. But Momo, being a bit of a magician, has turned the bakery into a restaurant.

Inside, it's all wood and warmth. Upstairs, it's a whole different scenario again: a place of calm, far from Ménilmontant, now one floor farther away, far from Oberkampf, where too much English is spoken. The menu is French, traditional, light. So light that you'll have room for one more beer. Across the street at Lou Pascalou, of course. Momo has invented his own Before and After.

Le Piston Pélican

15, RUE DE BAGNOLET, 20TH ARR.

☎ 01 43 70 35 00   🚇 ALEXANDRE-DUMAS

OPEN DAILY

THE PROBLEM WITH TRENDY BARS IS THAT THEY DON'T STAY THAT WAY FOR LONG—BY DEFINITION. THE PISTON Pélican has achieved the near-impossible: it's remained in fashion while becoming an institution in its corner of the 20th, a hangout for rock stars ever since the drummer of Telephone rented practice space in a nearby studio, l'Usine. They would come here to eat like pimps and drink like rebels, under the disquieting shadow of huge vats of wine, beer, and cider, relics of a time when this was a dry goods store and wine wholesaler.

There's no doubt that music has left its mark on the place. It was once the home of the brass band Le Piston Circus, after which the bar was named. Some say it used to be a whorehouse, too. It's anybody's guess.

In 1996, Franck brought a breath of fresh air into the place. He dusted off the musical selection, brought in electronica and DJ nights. All without sacrificing the populist energy that has soaked into the walls.

Lounging on the Métro-style benches, or sitting at the café tables across from one of the most beautiful zinc bars in Paris, a clientele of thirty-somethings tries to find the proper balance between the traditional and the modern.

It's exactly what Jean-Louis hoped for, when he took over the Piston. "A café that's both old…and new." This third-generation Auvergnat never thought he'd go into such a traditionally Auvergnat profession. But he couldn't resist the Pelican's beak. White wine and techno, pastis and punk. Jean-Louis, like his customers, is looking for the perfect balance.

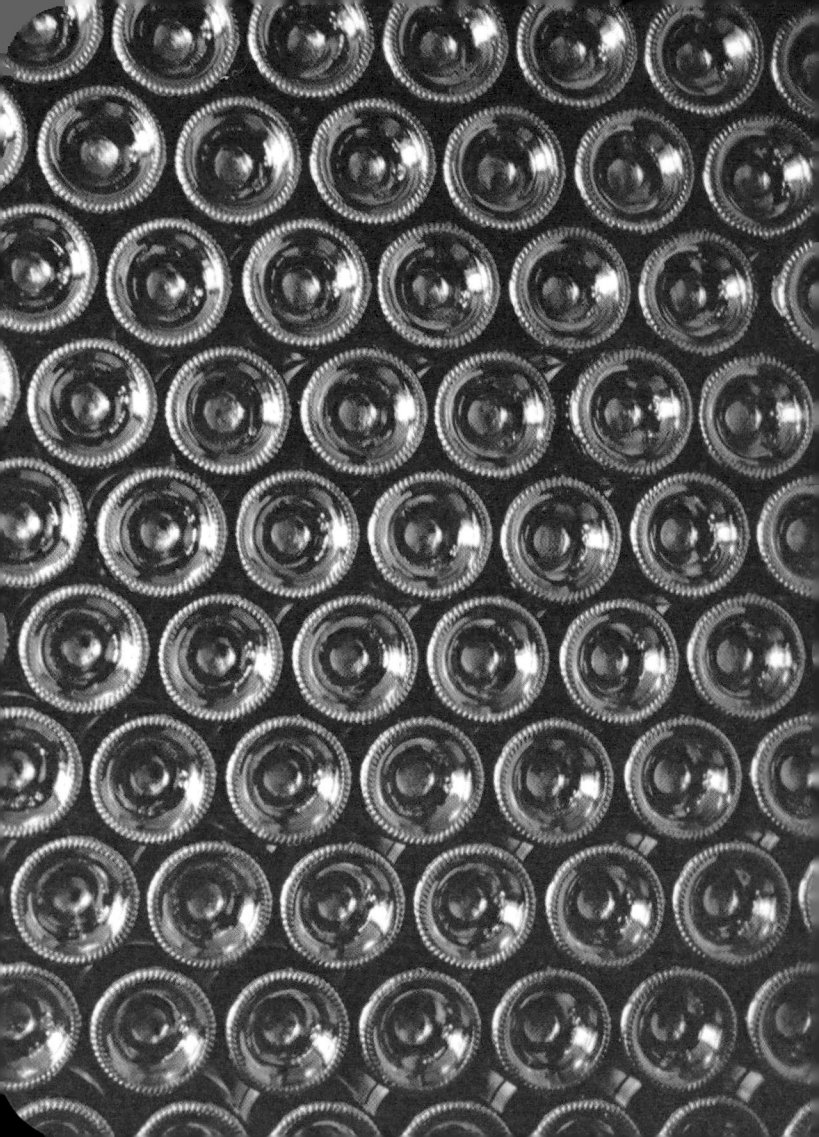

Index

Credits

FRANÇOIS THOMAZEAU is a sports writer, an author of detective novels, and an editor—three professions requiring inspiration and perspiration (and time spent in cafés).

SYLVAIN AGEORGES is a photographer specializing in Paris. He is the author of the *Guide to Jewish-Parisian Heritage* (Éditions Parigramme).

ANNA MOSCHOVAKIS is a poet and translator living in Brooklyn, NY. She is the author of *The Blue Book* (Phylum Press, 2005). An editor and book designer at Ugly Duckling Presse, she teaches in the Comparative Literature Department at Queens College.

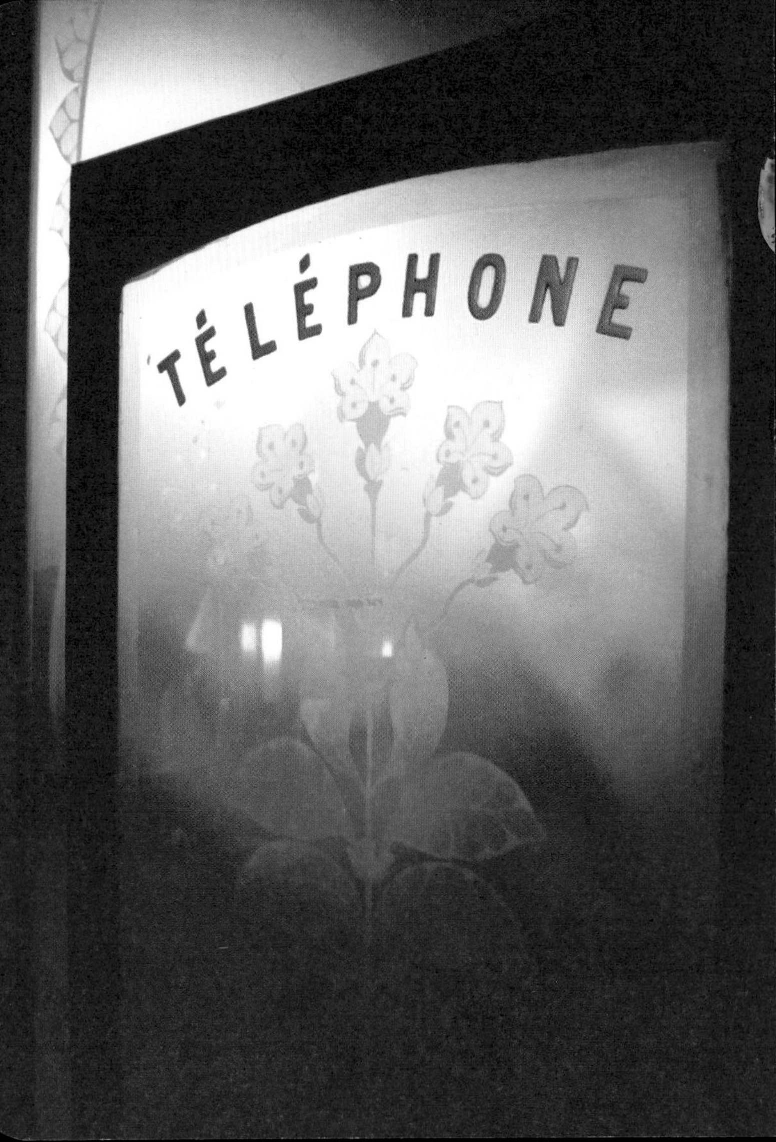
TÉLÉPHONE